WORDS
—— THAT ——
SELL

MORE THAN 6,000 ENTRIES TO HELP YOU PROMOTE YOUR PRODUCTS, SERVICES, AND IDEAS

REVISED AND EXPANDED EDITION

RICHARD BAYAN

McGRAW-HILL

New York   Chicago   San Francisco   Lisbon   London
Madrid   Mexico City   Milan   New Delhi
San Juan   Seoul   Singapore
Sydney   Toronto

12 13   QVS/QVS   15 14 13

ISBN 0-07-146785-8

This publication is designed to provide accurate and authoritative
information in regard to the subject matter covered. It is sold with
the understanding that the publisher is not engaged in rendering legal,
accounting, or other professional service. If legal advice or other expert
assistance is required, the services of a competent professional person
should be sought.

> —*From a declaration of principles jointly adopted by a committee*
> *of the American Bar Association and a committee of publishers.*

McGraw-Hill books are available at special quantity discounts to use
as premiums and sales promotions, or for use in corporate training
programs. For more information, please write to the Director of
Special Sales, Professional Publishing, McGraw-Hill, Two Penn Plaza,
New York, NY 10121-2298. Or contact your local bookstore.

 This book is printed on recycled, acid-free paper containing
a minimum of 50% recycled, de-inked fiber.

To the memory of my parents,
Aris and Chaqué Bayan,
with love and gratitude.

CONTENTS

Part 3 Clinchers

PREFACE

Like magicians with their props or fishermen with their time-tested lures, advertising copywriters rely upon a handy assortment of contrivances for seducing an audience. A copywriter's tools are words, and the most effective tools are words that *sell*. Infallible adjectives like *luxurious* and *irresistible*. Ageless phrases like *a lifetime of satisfaction* and *right at your fingertips*. And, of course, that sturdy old standard, *FREE!*

This volume represents an attempt to gather the most potent of these words and phrases into a single sourcebook. To compile this material, I rummaged through mountainous stacks of magazines, newspapers, direct-mail packages, and catalogs. I kept an ear open for compelling phrases that I heard over the radio and on television. I checked my e-mail for the occasional gold nugget embedded in the spam. I raided my own copy files, consulted more than one thesaurus, and, after organizing the entries into lists, added still more words and phrases as they came to mind. I rejected those entries that seemed to fall flat in print, and I shunned any slogans that were closely identified with specific products.

Think of this book as your personal magic kit—or, if you prefer, a bottomless tackle box filled with glittering lures. Use it whenever you require inspiration on short notice. Browse through its lists at leisure to expand your repertoire. With this book at your side, you'll be able to go straight to the words and phrases that suit your needs. Instead of groping for words, your mind will be free to focus on the real task of advertising and other promotional writing: shaping a message that generates an enthusiastic response from your audience.

ACKNOWLEDGMENTS

During my formative years as an advertising copywriter, I thought it might be a wise idea to compile a notebook of words and phrases to help me in my work. I toyed with the notion and let it pass.

Then a strange thing happened: somebody offered to *pay* me for compiling such a notebook. Motivated by the prospect of fame and riches, I set to work, produced a boxful of note cards, and emerged with the first edition of this book (which I finally did get to use in my work).

Roughly 20 years later, my publisher approached me about creating an updated edition of *Words That Sell*. I would like to thank the people who helped make this "new and improved" edition a reality: my editor, Monica Bentley, who offered me this project and remained gracious even through the deadline crunch; Pattie Amoroso, the kind of editing supervisor with whom every writer hopes to work; copyeditor Alice Manning and proofreader Frances Koblin, for their scrupulous attention to detail; production supervisor Cheryl Hudson, who helped turn a stack of pages into a handsome book; LaShae Ortiz, who designed the eye-catching cover; and marketing manager Seth Morris, with whose help (and a little luck) this edition of *Words That Sell* will reach even more readers than its predecessor.

I would also like to thank my wife, Anne, for her priceless love and support, and for letting me spread this project over the entire surface of our dining room table for nearly three months. Our son, Guy, who was a toddler when I compiled this edition, deserves a fatherly nod simply for being his delightful self.

I should also acknowledge, once again, all those nameless writers of advertisements, brochures, catalogs, and sales letters whose collective opus furnished me with so much of my raw material. Your work might not carry a byline, but it doesn't go unnoticed or unappreciated.

INTRODUCTION TO THE
SECOND EDITION

Those of us who write reference books enjoy a special privilege denied to practitioners of fiction. Unlike novelists and short story writers, we're free to keep revising and improving our work after it has made its debut in print.

Just try to imagine a second edition of *David Copperfield* or *The Great Gatsby* with "twice as many pages . . . hundreds of vivid new phrases . . . dozens of additional characters . . . intriguing new plot developments . . . new surprise ending!" Not on your life! But a book like *Words That Sell* was the perfect candidate for just such a revision.

Not for Copywriters Only. When I completed the first edition back in 1984, I was satisfied that I had created a useful little idea starter for my fellow advertising copywriters. But within months of the book's publication, it became obvious that this was no mere thesaurus for professional scribes like me. Word of *Words That Sell* spread rapidly throughout the advertising and marketing fields. It made its way into the hands of entrepreneurs, public relations professionals, sales reps and their managers, CEOs, corporate team builders, motivational experts, and, most recently, Webmasters with sites to promote.

Probably the most gratifying moment for me came when the new president of our company made his first tour around the building. Not knowing who I was, he remarked: "I see you have a copy of *Words That Sell* on your desk. That's one of my favorite books." (I should add that our relationship deteriorated from there.)

The Need for Revision. My little phrase book had made its mark. But I wasn't content. When I wrote the first edition, I was a young copywriter toiling for modest wages at a Long Island publishing company. I'm not sure I knew the difference between a product feature and a benefit in those days. As I matured and gained more knowledge in my field, I longed to create a more comprehensive version of *Words That Sell* that could function as a serious reference tool. Now I've been granted the opportunity to do just that. Let me tell you what I've done.

Nearly Twice as Many Entries as Before. If you have the first edition around for comparison, you'll notice that the new *Words That Sell* has more *words*. Lots more of them. With nearly twice as many entries at your disposal, you're nearly twice as likely to find a word or phrase that hits the mark. Yet we've managed to add all those new entries without significantly expanding the bulk (or the cost) of the book. How did we do it? The first edition had an abundance of white space, which may have been pleasing to the eye but sometimes gave the impression of skimpiness. For the second edition, we sacrificed some of that white space and simply packed more words onto each page.

At the same time, I've been careful not to go overboard in adding new entries. When you need quick inspiration, you don't want to scour a list that's as long as the Declaration of Independence. I've tried to maintain a healthy balance between inclusiveness and brevity, which is sort of like trying to be a moderate on the issue of vegetarianism. I hope I've succeeded in offering you an optimum number of entries for each list.

New Lists of Words and Phrases. I've made the existing lists longer, yes, but I've also added new ones where I thought the book needed them. For example, the old edition had no lists to convey the concepts of "competitive," "fast," and "good-looking" (to name three qualities that we as a culture have come to prize, for better or worse). I've added these lists and many more under "Descriptions and Benefits," the main section of the book.

I've also beefed up the "Grabbers" section with a long list of lively envelope teasers that shout, "Open me!" And I've enhanced the "Clinchers" section with lists of phrases to use in your *call to action, P.S.,* and *lift note.*

A Minor Reorganization. If you own the first edition, you'll see that I've deleted the section formerly known as "Terms and Offers." Maybe *deleted* is the wrong word: I've actually broken it up and redistributed its lists under "Grabbers" and "Clinchers," where they probably belonged in the first place. Now the book has only four sections of lists instead of five, and it should be that much easier to find your way around. I've also broken up some of the old lists ("Reliable/Solid," for example) wherever I thought the two conjoined concepts really called for two separate lists.

Updated Language. You'd expect the language of advertising to have changed radically since I compiled the first edition. After all, during that time we've moved from "Please don't squeeze the Charmin" to the upscale retro-posturing of the late J. Peterman catalog to the age of hip-hop and beyond. But the words that motivate the human spirit have remained relatively constant. We're still obsessed with status, security, comfort, fear, convenience, money, and all the other primal preoccupations of our species throughout the centuries.

The shift in our selling language since the first edition has been subtle but still noticeable: There's more informality, especially in letters and brochures. More contractions. Fewer dependent clauses and other complicated syntax. Not as much earnest paternal lecturing and a little more attitude. Fewer exclamation points. (After all, most of us want to appear cool, and it's not cool to exclaim. All those exclamation points look like little droplets of sweat on the forehead.)

I've loosened up the language in *Words That Sell*, but I haven't gone out of my way to tailor it to this year's fashions. You'll notice the occasional "extreme" or "slam-dunk," but for the most part we're still looking at classic selling language. In fact, I've kept most of the earnest old phrases that edgy copywriters at "boutique" agencies would dismiss as hopeless clichés (including "works like magic" and "right at your fingertips," to name a few hoary veterans that still pack a potent punch). But I've finally weeded out others that were starting to sound like relics of the Eisenhower administration. Does anyone still say *Seeing is believing*? Maybe in a few scattered nursing homes.

Now It's Up to You. So there you have it: a revised, enhanced, updated, slightly reorganized, and significantly expanded edition of *Words That Sell*—a book with roughly twice the power of its predecessor to enliven your copy and convert browsers into buyers. The surprising popularity of *Words That Sell* over the years has shown me that you don't always need to hire an ad agency to create effective advertising. You don't even need to be a professional writer. What matters is that you have the desire to sell from the heart, the savvy to reach your audience, and the determination to succeed. That and a good thesaurus will help you go miles toward accomplishing your goals. I'm happy that you've bought the new edition of *Words That Sell*. I hope you use it regularly and profitably.

HOW TO USE THIS BOOK

At some time in your life, you've probably used a thesaurus—a reference book filled with lists of synonyms. *Words That Sell* is a thesaurus of words and phrases used in advertising and other promotional writing. As in any standard thesaurus, the entries are organized by topic. Look up "Stylish," for example, and you'll find terms like *elegant* and *smashing*. Under "Convenient" you'll encounter *easily accessible* and *take it anywhere*. But this book departs from the usual thesaurus in several respects:

- *Words That Sell* is organized into sections that correspond with the natural progression of sales literature from beginning to end:

  1. **GRABBERS:** the teasers, headlines, slogans, opening statements, provocative questions, and other attention-getters that pull your audience into your message.

  2. **DESCRIPTIONS AND BENEFITS:** the words and phrases used to convey the compelling qualities of your product or service. This is by far the largest section of the book, and you'll probably be spending most of your time here.

  3. **CLINCHERS:** the persuasive closing statements (including guarantees and ordering information) that can push an undecided reader over the response threshold.

     The fourth section, "Special Strategies," is packed with aggressive words and phrases for specialized purposes, from "Flattering the Reader" to "Selling Your Ideas."

- In each of the four main sections, you'll find lists of words and phrases organized by topic. If you want to convey the idea of "big," for example, go to the section "Descriptions and Benefits" and find the topic "Big/Many." There you'll see a long list of words and phrases that you can use. If you're looking for an intriguing question to lead off your copy, turn to the section "Grabbers" and find "Opening with a Question." The table of contents gives you the complete list of sections and topics.

- The words and phrases under each topic aren't necessarily synonyms—they're simply useful expressions gathered in one place to help you express the idea you have in mind. Under "Sensory

Qualities," for example, you'll come across words as disparate as *ripe* and *windswept*. Yet you'll probably notice that similar expressions tend to gravitate together within a given list so that you can find what you need quickly and easily.

- Many of the phrases contain blanks or trail off in an ellipsis (. . .). For example:

Only _____ gives you . . .

Here you've been supplied with the pattern for a phrase, which you can easily adapt to your needs by filling in the missing word and extending the phrase as you see fit.

A few words of advice before you start: for best results, familiarize yourself with the four-part format of *Words That Sell*. That way you'll know just where to look for the topics you want. If one list doesn't yield a word or phrase that nails your idea, use the cross-references ("For further inspiration, see:") at the bottom of each list to continue your search elsewhere. The key word index at the back of the book will help you go to the right place if you can't find a list that suits your idea.

Even this expanded edition of *Words That Sell* doesn't pretend to be exhaustive. In the coming months and years, as in the past, I'm sure I'll stumble across words and phrases that would have made first-rate entries. No doubt you will, too. When you find them, why not write them down under the appropriate topic and expand the collection. In time, my book will become your book—and that's the way it was meant to be.

A CRASH COURSE
IN COPYWRITING

An advertising copywriter uses words as tools to persuade and motivate an audience. You persuade your readers that you have something valuable to offer; you motivate them to acquire it for themselves. This is the essence of effective advertising, whether you opt for the hard sell or the subliminal suggestion.

The following guidelines, distilled from my own experience and that of other professional copywriters, should help you avoid some of the hobgoblins to which members of our tribe too often fall prey. At the same time—and with a minimum of trial and error—you'll gain the perspective you need to start peppering your writing with "words that sell."

BEFORE YOU WRITE

1. **Gain firsthand knowledge of your product or service.** Do a little research to get your facts straight. Gather your data from current sources of information (marketing fact sheets, product managers, recent copy). If it's the kind of product you can hold in your hands (or read or taste or listen to), go right ahead. Live with it for a while and get the feel of it. Then look at your product or service as if you were the consumer. What features and benefits would attract *you* as a prospective customer?

2. **"Position" your product or service.** How is it different from or superior to the competition? Who would use it? How would you define it in a single phrase? Positioning is critical if you want to develop a competitive (and ultimately successful) marketing strategy.

3. **Know your audience.** Always gear your copy to the needs and tastes of your customers. Are they mass-market consumers? Upscale young professionals? Hard-boiled professional buyers with a bottom-line mentality? Executives in your field? Find out by checking the demographics of the media in which you'll be advertising, or (in the case of direct mail) by obtaining a breakdown of your mailing lists.

4. **Plan your copy strategy.** Decide how much copy you'll need to convey the message. As a general rule of thumb (especially in catalogs), the length of your copy should vary in proportion to your company's investment in the product. But not always. If your product is simple and its virtues self-evident, you don't have much explaining to do. Other points worth considering: Do you want to develop a running theme that serves as a conceptual focal point for your copy? Do you want to advertise a line of related products? And be sure to coordinate your plans with the designer so that you're both working with the same concept in mind.

WHEN YOU WRITE

1. **Don't lose sight of your primary goal: to sell your product or service.** Your writing should be more than a flat presentation of the facts. (Remember that a copywriter must persuade and motivate.) On the other hand, don't let runaway creativity bury the message. The most brilliant efforts will be wasted if your audience can't remember what product you're pushing. Write to sell.

2. **Stress the benefits.** Resist the temptation to thump your chest on behalf of your company. It's not "See how great we are," but "See what we can do for you." Show your potential customers how your product or service will make them happier, wealthier, more comfortable, or more secure. Write with their interests in mind. Once you make the transition from company-centered copy to customer-centered copy, that's half the battle.

3. **Arouse interest.** From the headline to the ordering statements, your copy should continually pique the reader's curiosity. As you unfold the benefits, keep seasoning your copy with human interest, helpful tips, curious facts, colorful phrases—anything to heighten involvement in your story. And write so that your audience actually looks forward to hearing from you again—an accomplishment that means more in the long run than a one-time sale.

4. **Don't fill your copy with empty overstatements.** Too many words like *fabulous* and *fantastic* within a brief space will destroy your credibility. You don't want your audience to dismiss you as a propagandist. Instead, try to *convince* the audience that your product is fabulous. Make *them* say, "That's really fantastic!"

5. **Be accurate.** Be sure you get the facts straight. Don't leave yourself open to claims of false advertising by making statements that can't be substantiated. Above all, be truthful. Resist the temptation to distort the facts in pursuit of an easy sale.

6. **Be specific.** Don't use hazy abstractions or approximations when you have a chance to create vivid images with simple, observable details. Would you rather eat a "frozen dessert" or a "raspberry ice"? And try to avoid the notorious "than what?" comparisons—for example, "lasts longer" (than what?) or "gets the job done faster" (than what?). Do everything you can to sharpen the picture.

7. **Be organized.** Your message should progress logically from the headline to the clincher. Don't bury essential information in the darkest recesses of your copy or lead off with trivia that stops the reader cold. Like an old-fashioned short story, your copy should have a beginning, a middle, and an end.

8. **Write for easy reading.** Your style should suit the audience you're addressing, but certain rules apply to all copy. Cultivate a style that flows smoothly and rapidly, a style that's clear, uncluttered, involving, and persuasive. Avoid long, convoluted sentence constructions. Affect a crisp but friendly and extroverted tone. Communicate. You want to do everything possible to ensure that your message gets read.

9. **Appeal to the emotions rather than the intellect.** You want your words to propel the reader to action, and nothing is so propulsive as human emotions. A cerebral approach might make your reader nod in admiration, but emotions are the fuel that can blast your message off the ground. Even when you're writing for an audience of executives or college professors, don't forget that, like all members of the human tribe, they're motivated by gut feelings. Keep in mind that some advertising media are intrinsically less emotional than others. A brochure, for example, has to present the hard facts. It typically won't generate as much emotional heat as a good sales letter. But it should still trigger an emotional response ("I *want* that!").

10. **Don't offend.** Humor is a controversial issue among advertising insiders. Most direct-mail experts preach against it, but there's no denying that humor can be an effective tool—if it suits the subject or the situation. (You don't want to joke about insurance or funerals.) Sarcasm, cynicism, and

other extreme forms of individuality are not likely to meet with mass approval. Don't criticize your audience's taste in clothes, music, pets, or anything else. Don't preach. Be of a sunny disposition, and aim to please.

11. **Make use of testimonials and reviews.** Satisfied customers can supply you with some of your most persuasive copy, because their pronouncements invariably come from the heart. These folks have actually tested the product and witnessed the benefits firsthand, and they simply can't contain their enthusiasm. What better sales weapon could you ask for? Just be sure to obtain their permission first. If you have glowing reviews from publications or esteemed professionals in your field, be sure to quote them and display the blurbs in a prominent spot.

12. **Ask for the customer's order.** This is a sound practice, especially if you *want* the customer to order! Without a persuasive "call to action"—the brief, high-powered statement that impels prospective customers to buy and tells them how—you let your audience off the hook before you've closed the sale. They'll finish reading your letter or brochure, smile contentedly, and drift back to sleep.

13. **Revise and edit your work.** Cut out all dead wood; every word should pull its weight. (Advertising copy is like poetry in this respect.) Be your own critic. Check your facts, your syntax, your spelling. Make sure you haven't left anything out. Then read your copy again before you submit it.

CATEGORIES OF COPY

CATALOGS introduce your company's entire product line, or a preselected portion of the product line, in a booklet filled with compelling product descriptions. Copy should be kept brief, crisp, and to the point; the reader must have instant access to key facts. Lead off your entries with powerful adjectives and verbs; avoid beginning with a flat "This _____ is . . ." Sentence fragments are perfectly acceptable—almost mandatory. Products can be grouped by category, price range, or any other system that makes sense. The only rule about grouping is to be consistent throughout. It's generally a good idea to display related products together on a single page or spread; that way you'll encourage multiple purchases. The opening spread, back cover, and order form are considered valuable "real estate" for selling your products. Still, you might want to add a brief, upbeat introductory message about your company in one of these areas; a friendly exhortation from the president is almost always effective. The order form should be bound in, easy to understand, and easily detached.

SELF-MAILERS are aggressive, relatively low-cost selling tools that generally focus on a single product or a small range of products. Everything's there on one folded sheet: headlines, sell copy, visuals, call to action, guarantee, and order form. The ideal order form is a detachable return-response card, but a clip-out order coupon will do the job if you want to cut costs. Be sure to include your toll-free number and Web address in a highly visible location.

DIRECT-MAIL PACKAGES are the traditional workhorses of the advertising world: not the sort of medium that captures the public imagination, like a good TV ad campaign, but something even more admirable. These humble yet potent packages are filled with strategic devices that have been scientifically tested over *decades* to maximize consumer response. They're ideal for spotlighting a single important product or a related series of products. Key copy elements include:

The Envelope Teaser—a boisterous one-liner that compels the reader to tear open the package.
A teaser can be a tantalizing benefit ("FREE!"), a provocative question, or a juicy tidbit of information

that promises more tidbits inside. But don't ever promise something on the outside that you can't deliver inside. Try to resist the current temptation to shout "URGENT—REPLY REQUESTED!" on every mailing. After all, we don't want our public to grow more jaded than necessary. One more consideration: some experts contend that the best teaser is no teaser at all. (Your package will look more official and less like advertising.)

The Brochure—the folded, generally colorful broadside sheet that illustrates the merits of your product. Your copy should unfold in clear, logical prose, but the reader should be free to skip around and still absorb your message. Break up your copy into easily managed units with catchy subheads. Outstanding product features can be highlighted with bullets, callouts, or other visual attention getters. The photos and captions carry half the burden of selling your products.

The Sales Letter—potentially your most effective selling tool: personal and persuasive like a one-on-one sales pitch, yet without the intense pressure that can force customers to keep their guard up. Where the brochure typically appeals to the reader's intellect and curiosity, the letter must engage the emotions. Here's your opportunity to infuse your advertising with living, breathing *personality*. Adopt a natural, unstilted writing style that follows everyday speech patterns: no *as per*s, *herein*s, or *please find enclosed*s. The so-called Johnson box—a few boldface lines at the top to summarize your offer and entice the reader—is an effective response-boosting device. It takes some of the pressure off the opening paragraphs of your letter, so you can build a more leisurely personal argument without taxing the reader's patience. If you want, you can vary the paragraph widths as a visual gimmick to hold the reader's attention.

The Lift Note—the safety net of any direct-mail package. If your letter fails to convince your prospect, the folded lift note gives you a second chance. On the outside, you challenge readers with a provocative one-liner that compels them to look inside—especially if (as the typical lift note asserts) they've "already decided not to order." When they open the note, your concise, heartfelt message plays upon their guilt. "Frankly," you sigh, "I don't understand why only 2 or 3 percent of you will take us up on this risk-free offer." Then, in a few sentences, you sum up the compelling reasons to buy.

The Order Form—not to be underestimated as a powerful selling tool in its own right. A good order form sums up your offer, highlights the product's selling points, adds a compelling call to action, states your guarantee, displays your contact information, and provides space for the customer to order by mail. That's a lot of responsibility for one little card. In fact, many experts consider the order form to be the single most important element in a direct-mail package. So pay special attention when you create order form copy. Make it upbeat (Yes!) and irresistible.

BUCKSLIPS are miniature ads (their name comes from their traditional size: roughly the same dimensions as a dollar bill) that are sometimes inserted in a direct-mail package along with brochures and letters. Use them to advertise a related product or a special premium. You don't have much space to work with, so make your message loud and urgent.

STATEMENT STUFFERS are mini-brochures that are enclosed with invoices and other billing statements. Like buckslips, stuffers are limited by their diminutive size (and by the tendency of the recipient to chuck them away unread). You definitely have to shout to get attention. Use a dynamic "grabber" and crisp catalog-style copy with a simple order form on the back.

MAGALOGS are miniature magazines created and mailed by your organization. The good news is that you control both the advertising and the editorial content, so you can shape the entire publication as a subtle selling tool for your products. Your audience can involve itself in informative articles, colorful graphics, eye-catching sidebars, and other devices that heighten their involvement without subjecting them to relentless selling. The bad news is that magalogs are relatively expensive to produce and don't offer you as much active selling space as a catalog or brochure of the same size. But if you have a complicated product with an abundance of features that would benefit from a leisurely editorial-pictorial treatment, a magalog might be just the right vehicle.

SPACE ADS are simply the printed ads that fill most newspapers and magazines. They are as various as breeds of dogs—from the sleek wolfhounds of Madison Avenue to the plucky mutts that yelp for attention in the back pages of men's magazines. Yet successful space ads all share a few key traits: they grab the reader within seconds, they know their audience, and they convey a potent message within the confines of their allotted space. Large space ads tend to rely more on cool visuals than on earnest copy. The smaller the ad, the greater the importance of the copy (and the benefits). Copy is also paramount in direct-response space ads of all sizes. (Don't forget to include a persuasive call to action and contact information.)

COMMERCIALS are essentially space ads broadcast over the airwaves. Unlike most other forms of advertising, commercials give you the advantage of a captive audience. You're free to use humor if it suits your purpose (when was the last time you read a funny brochure?). Keep in mind that a well-written commercial follows the natural patterns of human speech; it pays to have a colleague read the copy aloud before you submit it. Direct-response commercials always include a call to action and the necessary contact information.

INFOMERCIALS are the televised equivalent of magalogs (see opposite). You grab a half hour of airtime (ideally in a low-cost, off-peak time slot), then build the entire show around your product. Everyone knows it's a commercial, of course, but if you provide enough entertainment value and information, you'll have a ready audience for your sales pitch. Like any direct-response advertising vehicle, an infomercial always culminates in a forceful call to action, with contact information prominently displayed and repeated for best results.

CARD DECKS are compact packets filled with dozens of ads on individual cards. When you write copy for a card deck, remember that your prospect is being bombarded with ads. Your copy must practically knock the reader over the head to be noticed. Grab your prospects with a short, punchy headline, then hit them instantly with the benefits and a strong call to action.

POSTCARDS are essentially miniature self-mailers. Unlike card decks, they don't force you to compete with 50 other shouting voices. But you still need to grab the reader quickly and assertively. They're quick and inexpensive—ideal for easy-to-explain products or as the first part of a multistep selling strategy (ask your reader to send for your catalog or log onto your Web site).

YOUR WEB SITE is just an online store, right? Think again. A good Web site is actually a powerful brand statement as well as an extended ad for your products or services. Like a magalog, it entices readers with information they can use . . . it involves them with your product line and motivates them to order from you. Unlike magalog copy, Web copy should be brisk and concise enough to hold an impatient audience. (Think of Web surfers as jackrabbits hopping around as their whims dictate.) On your home page especially, use pithy teaser statements to encourage your audience to click on each link. Use subheads to break up your copy, but not so many of them that you clutter the page. Give your site a distinct personality. Keep it professional, but don't try to sound like everybody else.

E-MAIL SALES LETTERS are probably the last refuge of long advertising copy in the electronic age. Your copy approach should mirror what you'd do for a printed sales letter: tell a compelling story, involve the reader, offer tangible benefits, and invite response with a persuasive call to action. E-mail letters offer a few key advantages over the paper-and-ink variety. They're cheap to create. They don't require postage. And they can link to your site—directly to the offer page, if you like. (What better response vehicle could you imagine?) The trick is to overcome the public resistance to spam, which, if possible, is even greater than the public resistance to "junk mail." (*Note:* Try to avoid sending unsolicited e-mails. Instead, gather your own list of prospects who click on your banner ads or register at your site. Your response rate should shoot skyward, and you won't have to worry about the spam police.)

E-ZINES (a.k.a. online newsletters) are among the cheapest and most effective media ever developed for nurturing that critical relationship with your customers. Think about it: you provide informative content that your customers look forward to reading, and you can relax from the hard-sell tone of your catalogs and sales letters. Your chatty, offbeat approach enables customers to let down their guard and get actively involved with your message. You can personalize your e-zines, test different offers, and gain new prospects through customer referrals. Sounds almost too good to be true. The key is to keep coming up with fresh, interesting content.

BANNER ADS are like miniature billboards that entice Web surfers to visit your site. With their flashing, blinking, gyrating graphics, you could almost compare them to seductive flames attracting moths in the night. The object, of course, is not to zap the visitor to a crisp but to generate a clicking response. Though it seems obvious, you should always include the words "Click here" on a banner ad. Display your URL, too—just to impress it on the prospect's mind with repeat viewings. That doesn't leave much room for creative copy, of course. But an animated ad gives you two or three shots at persuading the viewer. A good banner ad creates instant awareness of your site, and you can select a targeted plan that shows your ad only to prospects who click on related subjects.

POP-UP ADS are the scourge of the Internet: pesky intruders that suddenly superimpose themselves over Web site content that you're trying to read. I don't know anyone who likes them, and they hurt our cause by contributing to the general public's disdain for advertising. See if you can avoid creating them. If we're lucky, they'll be an endangered species by the time you read this.

POSTERS AND POINT-OF-PURCHASE DISPLAYS are simply "grabbers" displayed in stores to catch the consumer's attention and motivate impulse buying. Remember that your display will be competing against dozens of other units in a vast battleground of products.

BILLBOARDS are roadside grabbers. Let the visual image sell the product, and keep the verbiage to an absolute minimum. After all, your audience has only a second or two to catch your message, and you don't want to cause any accidents.

PRESS RELEASES or **NEWS RELEASES** announce your message to the news media, which in turn will (you hope) disseminate it to the public. Whether sent by e-mail or snail mail, a good press release is "newsy" above all else; the editor who reads it is looking for material that will make a lively story. Get attention with a powerful headline and a banner that reads "For immediate release" (or something equally urgent). But remember to maintain a reasonably sober journalistic voice throughout the piece. Wildly enthusiastic press releases without editorial substance are dismissed as "puffery" by seasoned pros. And puffery invariably ends up in the wastebasket. Try to contain your story on a page or two. Don't feel obligated to spell out every detail; you want the editor to call you, after all. (That's why you've provided all that contact information at the top of the page.)

PART I

GRABBERS

MAKING THE READER
SIT UP AND
TAKE NOTICE

TEASERS

Free!
Absolutely free!
Free gift
Free gift enclosed
Valuable gift enclosed*
Your free _____ is enclosed
Free download!
Claim your free _____
Check enclosed
Free trial
No-risk trial offer
_____-day free trial offer
No obligation ever!
Exclusive offer
Exclusive offer for _____ members only
Limited-time offer
Introductory offer
Special get-acquainted offer
For a limited time only
_____ days only
Dated material
Send no money
Risk-free opportunity
Money-making opportunity
You have been selected to . . .
A _____ has been reserved in your name
Win . . .
Save . . .
Get a . . .

Bonus offer
Rebate offer
Urgent*
Important
Important update
Official documents enclosed*
Valuable document enclosed*
Valuable coupons enclosed
Priority mail enclosed*
_____ enclosed
Enclosed: _____
Inside: _____
Re: _____
Here is the information you requested*
Immediate reply requested*
Your signature is required*
Please respond within _____ days*
Sign the enclosed _____ right away
Last chance!*
Final notice*
A personal message from _____
An urgent message for _____*
Photos inside
Please do not bend
Do not bend or fold
Attention
New!
New offer
Introducing . . .

Announcing . . .
As seen on TV
Back by popular demand
Price break!
Prices slashed!
$_____ in savings enclosed
$_____ coupon enclosed
Save _____% on _____!
Take an extra _____% off!
Lowest prices ever*
New low price!
Price blowout!
Outrageous deal
Sale
Spring _____ sale
Summer _____ sale
Fall _____ sale

Winter _____ sale
Private sale
Members-only sale
Members-only discount
Special discount
Grand opening
Good news!
Great news!
Sneak preview!
Your _____ is about to expire
Imagine life without _____
_____ reasons to . . .
_____ things they never tell you about _____
_____ facts you should know about _____
Startling news about _____
Details inside . . .

*Note: Please use these statements only if you honestly believe they're true. Nobody likes to be hoodwinked into opening an envelope or e-mail. For this reason, I've omitted deceptive teasers like *Your Winning Ticket Is Enclosed!* and *Please Do Not Discard*. (Smart consumers know that the latter phrase screams "JUNK MAIL!") Even *urgent* is losing its urgency as readers grow more jaded. There are plenty of honest ways to hook a reader.

For further inspiration, see:
Free/Prize
Sale/Discount
All-Purpose Grabbers
Money-Saving (Part 2)

FREE / PRIZE

yours free
absolutely free
free of charge
at no charge
Valuable gift enclosed!
Free gift!
Free gift enclosed!
Free gift with purchase!
Free download!
Free CD!
Free catalog!
Free course!
Free sample!
Buy one, get one free.
We're giving away . . .
It's yours to keep.
Keep it, use it, enjoy it!
Keep it with our compliments.
It's your bonus for ordering now.
It's our gift to you.
Accept this _____.
You'll also receive a _____ at no extra charge.
Send for free facts.
This one's on us!

Included at no extra cost
No hidden fees
No annual fee
A $_____ value—absolutely free!
A $_____ value—yours free!
It's yours free just for saying "yes" to _____.
Take it—it's yours!
It's our way of saying "thank you."
Claim your free _____!
We'll reserve your bonus gift.
Early bird bonus
Win . . .
Win a brand-new _____!
Play and win!
Double your winnings!
Over _____ chances to win!
Take your pick of these fabulous prizes:
Hundreds of prizes!
All prizes will be awarded!

For further inspiration, see:
Teasers
All-Purpose Grabbers
Money-Saving (Part 2)

SALE/DISCOUNT

Save up to _____%

_____% off!

_____% discount!

Price break!

Price blowout!

Prices slashed!

New low price!

We've rolled back prices.

We've cut our prices on _____.

Drastic reductions on _____.

Take an extra _____% off the ticketed price!

One-day sale!

One day only!

Shop till you drop!

Winter/Spring/Summer/Fall preview/clearance sale

Preseason sale

Back-to-school sale

Warehouse sale

Every _____ on sale!

Private sale

Exclusive members-only sale

Giant closeout sale!

Final clearance!

Everything must go!

We must move our inventory.

A steal at these prices!

Value priced at $_____.

Prices guaranteed through _____.

Take advantage of this offer while it lasts.

Biggest discounts anywhere!

No lower prices anywhere!

We challenge you to find lower prices anywhere.

We challenge you to find a _____ at a lower price.

Lowest prices/rates allowed by law!

Guaranteed lowest prices!

We will not be undersold.

We will beat any price.

Don't pay more!

Comparable _____s currently sell for $_____ or more.

. . . at a substantial savings you can't afford to pass up.

Carnival of savings!

Save big on _____.

Buy more, save more!

Check our quantity discounts!

huge discounts

extra savings

tremendous savings

substantial savings

unbeatable value

Compare prices!

Shop and compare!

For further inspiration, see:

Teasers

Free/Prize

Money-Saving (Part 2)

TRIAL OFFER/
NO OBLIGATION

Send no money now!

Send no payment now!

Send no money!

No risk now, no risk later.

No-risk trial offer

30-day free trial

No obligation to buy anything ever!

No strings attached!

Use it for a week in your own home.

You may cancel at any time.

Say "yes" now and decide later.

If you decide to keep it, pay just $ _____.

If I decide to keep it, I will pay just $_____.

Choose only the _____ you want.

Keep only the _____ you want.

You may cancel at any time, simply by notifying us.

If you decide to cancel, pay nothing and keep
   the _____ with our compliments.

No purchase necessary!

No down payment!

totally refundable

No salesperson will call.

Try us for six months.

All we're asking is that you give us a try.

a fair trial

Try us on for size.

What have you got to lose?

Try _____ at our risk.

We'll buy it back—no questions asked.

We'll send you _____ to examine FREE—no cost,
   obligation, or commitment.

For further inspiration, see:
Guarantees (Part 3)
Persuading Your Audience (Part 3)

HEADS AND SLOGANS

Switch to _____.

Success starts with _____.

The _____ that works as hard as you do.

It's time for _____.

_____ spoken here!

The truth about your _____ could shock you.

Turn your _____ into a _____.

How do you turn a _____ into a _____?

_____ doesn't have to be expensive.

_____ fever!

A little _____ can go a long way.

Get comfortable with _____.

Power up your _____.

Turbocharge your _____.

How our _____ stacks up against theirs.

Not just another _____.

The _____ that makes other _____s look like toys.

Don't settle for _____ when you can choose _____.

Why your first _____ should be a _____.

The _____ advantage.

The _____ edge.

Your partner in _____.

A _____ for all seasons.

Taste/See/Hear/Feel the difference yourself!

Only _____ gives you . . .

The best-kept secret in _____.

_____ secrets revealed!

They don't call us _____ for nothing.

Always go to an expert.

We don't cut corners.

It takes more than talent.

The _____ experts.

The _____'s best friend.

At _____ , you're #1.

Get hooked on _____.

Go with a winner.

A winner never quits.

It's easy to spot the winners.

It's easy to see . . .

Meet the newest addition to our family.

Announcing the first _____ that . . .

Introducing the _____ that practically runs itself.

Introducing the _____ of the future.

The best _____ just became affordable.

You probably thought you couldn't afford a _____.

Are you paying too much for _____?

First-class _____ at no-frills prices.

The price cutters.

The dependables.

America's #1_____.

America's favorite _____.

_____'s favorite _____.

The _____ pledge.

A major breakthrough in _____.

Innovation is a tradition at _____.

Built to last.

The fun begins with _____.

Instant _____.

_____ in your pocket.

_____ legally!

The smart choice.

Success tool.

Management tool.

Executives only.

The right address.

Money in the bank.

Ever dependable.

Genius at work.

Child's play.

Your move.
Sinful.
Shocking.
Electrifying.
Legend.
Food for thought.
All the right ingredients.
Some cold, hard facts.
Inside information.
Fiction: (. . .). Fact: (. . .).
Get all the facts about _____.
Straight talk about _____.
Let's be honest about _____.
The startling truth about _____.
Everything you always wanted
    to know about _____.
_____ things you should
    never . . .
_____ things you should
    always . . .
What they never tell you
    about _____.
What they don't want you to
    know about _____.
Welcome to the _____ Age.
Don't get stuck with . . .

_____ where you want it, when
    you want it.
Finally, there's a better way to . . .
Nothing sells like a _____.
Nothing's built like a _____.
Nothing works like a _____.
The only _____ you'll ever need.
The last _____ you'll ever need
    to buy.
There's no substitute for _____.
In a class by itself.
Your satisfaction is our business.
_____ is our business.
_____ means business.
_____ can handle it.
The _____ that never quits.
Don't gamble with . . .
Don't take chances with . . .
Say good riddance to _____.
Say yes to _____.
A _____ from the word "go."
Who says you can't win 'em all?
For those special times.
For those special people in your life.
Give your children the _____ they
    deserve.

An investment in their future.
An investment in your future.
Now, more than ever, you
    need _____.
_____ reasons you should . . .
Can you afford not to . . .?
You have better things to do
    than . . .
Don't wait for _____ to come
    to you!
Don't make these _____ mistakes
    when you _____.
Take a minute to . . .
Your shortcut to . . .
Turn your life around!
Train for the future.
Turn your free time into learning
    time.
_____ with confidence.
You owe yourself a _____.
All the _____ you need to succeed.

*For other heads and slogans, see
individual topics throughout the
book.*

SALUTATIONS AND INVITATIONS

Dear Friend:

Dear Neighbor:

Dear Customer:

Dear Preferred Customer:

Dear Valued Customer:

Dear _____ Client:

Dear Buyer:

Dear _____ Fan:

Dear _____ Fanatic:

Dear _____ Aficionado:

Dear _____ Connoisseur:

Dear _____ Enthusiast:

Dear _____ Lover:

Dear _____ Buff:

Dear _____ Collector:

Dear Patron of the Arts:

Dear Reader:

Dear Shareholder:

Dear Investor:

Dear Subscriber:

Dear Retailer:

Dear Member:

Dear Citizen:

Dear Concerned Citizen:

Dear Achiever:

Dear Classmate:

Dear Fellow _____:

Greetings!

Attention!

Welcome to . . .

Come with us . . .

You are cordially invited . . .

A special invitation . . .

A personal invitation . . .

You're about to join . . .

Get ready to enjoy . . .

We request your presence . . .

You've been selected . . .

Your name has appeared on our select
    list of _____s.

Join us . . .

We want you to . . .

Try this on for size:

Special information for _____s only.

For further inspiration, see:
Flattering the Reader (Part 4)

OPENING WITH A QUESTION

Isn't it time you . . .?

When was the last time you . . .?

Did you know that . . .?

Are you still . . .?

Want to keep in touch with . . .?

Want to stay abreast of . . .?

Are you interested in . . .?

Are you curious about . . .?

Are you intrigued by . . .?

Will you be ready for the . . .?

Who could say no to . . .?

What's the best investment you could make?

Could you use an extra $ _____ each month?

Do you want a better job?

How secure is your job?

Why postpone your future in . . .?

What would you say if we offered to help you . . .?

Will you risk just $1 to . . .?

Have you ever stayed awake at night thinking
  about . . .?

Do you ever ask yourself . . .?

How many times have you said to yourself, . . .?

Has this ever happened to you?

How long has it been since you . . .?

Remember the first time you ever . . .?

Are you secretly afraid of . . .?

Don't you need . . .?

Don't you wish . . .?

Wouldn't you like to . . .?

Looking for just the right _____?

Confused about which _____ to buy?

Why should you use _____ when you can . . .?

Tired of empty promises from . . .?

Tired of the same old _____?

Why trade a _____ for a _____?

Why sacrifice _____ for _____?

Are you ready for . . .?

Who can put a price on _____?

Why pay full price for _____?

Are you paying too much for _____?

Want to stretch your purchasing power?

How can you cut the high cost of _____?

How much is your company spending on _____?

Are you drowning in a sea of _____?

Have you ever thought about . . .?

What's the most effective way to . . .?

What's the most profitable . . .?

What's the safest . . .?

Do you enjoy _____?

OPENING WITH
A STATEMENT

It's no secret that . . .

Let me ask you a simple question.

We'll change your mind about . . .

You've probably noticed that . . .

Just wait until you . . .

I'm extremely pleased to tell you that . . .

The results are in.

Recent research shows that . . .

It's not every day that . . .

Here's an idea worth considering.

Forget everything you've heard about . . .

Imagine being able to get a _____ for only $_____.

Just a note to tell you about . . .

Don't let _____ keep you from getting ahead.

Don't be caught without _____.

_____ often spells the difference between failure and success.

Within 30 days, you could be . . .

You can organize a successful _____.

Think about . . .

Now you can . . .

For under $_____ you can . . .

If I'm not mistaken, you're the kind of person who . . .

As a _____, you know how important it is to . . .

Believe it or not, . . .

You're in for a pleasant surprise.

If you're like most people, you probably . . .

If _____ is your passion, then you'll appreciate . . .

In today's competitive market-place, . . .

In today's uncertain economy, . . .

In today's volatile market, . . .

_____ industry experts estimate that . . .

We live in an increasingly complex society.

Today, more than ever, . . .

It's a fact of life that . . .

It's never too early to . . .

It's never too late to . . .

Now, the real truth about _____.

I used to think that . . .

Sometimes I wonder why . . .

I've taken the liberty of reserving a _____ in your name.

Let's talk about why you need _____.

Your new career in _____ is just weeks away.

Anyone who knows _____ will tell you that . . .

It isn't enough to be . . .

Every once in a while you come across a _____ that . . .

_____ could determine the future of your business.

If you've been waiting for the right _____, you don't have to wait any longer.

It's hard enough to _____ without having to worry about _____.

Let's be honest.

Let's face it.

We've got the solution to your . . .

In the few seconds it took you to read this far, . . .

If you'd like to become part of today's _____ , there's no better way to start than . . .

For further inspiration, see:
Heads and Slogans

OPENING WITH A CHALLENGE

Get ready to . . .
Prepare yourself for . . .
Take a giant step . . .
Fasten your seatbelt!
Watch out!
Beware!
Put your _____ to the test.
Test yourself . . .
Challenge yourself . . .
Match yourself against . . .
Delve into the . . .
Visit the . . .
Take off for . . .
Leap into the . . .
Dive into the . . .
Discover the . . .
Explore the . . .
Encounter the . . .
Experience the . . .
Meet the . . .
Learn about the . . .
Say "yes" to . . .
Join the . . .
Capture the . . .
Recapture the . . .
Relive the . . .
Savor the . . .

Cross the threshold . . .
Climb aboard . . .
Scale a new peak . . .
Plumb the depths of . . .
If you're bold enough . . .
Take a deep breath and . . .
Do something extraordinary:
Let your imagination soar!
Dare to live your dreams.
You already have what it takes to win.
Be your own (mechanic, plumber, etc.).
If you think you're good enough . . .
If you're seriously interested in . . .
If you consider yourself . . .
If you sincerely want to . . .
For once in your life, . . .
Join the small handful of people who . . .
_____ like a professional.
_____ like an expert.
_____ like a millionaire.
_____ like the person you were meant to be.
I think you'll be shocked by what you're
    about to read.

For further inspiration, see:
Self-Improvement (Part 2)

SNAPPY TRANSITIONS

Now, for the first time, . . .
Now there's an even better way to . . .
That's where _____ fits in.
Think of it:
Imagine:
Fortunately, . . .
Here's why:
Here's how:
Here's how it works:
What I'm leading up to is this:
I'm hoping you fall into that category.
I'd like to call your attention to . . .
If questions like these intrigue you . . .
But first, . . .
If you prefer, . . .
You'll be surprised to learn that . . .
We're about to change all that.
What does this mean for you?
To be perfectly honest, . . .
Simply stated, . . .
In short, . . .
In brief, . . .
Let me explain.
But let's take a closer look.
Look at our track record:
That's a claim very few _____s can make.
What an opportunity!
I'm sure you'll agree that . . .
One thing is for sure:

This we promise:
Come to think of it, . . .
To show you what I mean, . . .
For the answer, turn this page.
As you can see, . . .
As you might imagine, . . .
No doubt about it, . . .
Obviously, . . .
Here are just a few of the . . .
These are just a few of the . . .
For these and many other reasons . . .
You'll also be glad to know that . . .
As a further convenience, . . .
Here's a better solution:
And here's an added feature:
And this is only the beginning!
All this and more!
And that's not all.
And there's more:
As if that's not enough, . . .
And we don't stop there.
And don't overlook . . .
But there's even more.
But before I say any more, . . .
But that's just part of the story.
And this is only a small sampling.
The result?
Sounds incredible?
Sounds fantastic?

A miracle?
Fair enough?
No problem!
You bet!
. . . and that's the truth.
The truth is, . . .
But look—
The way I look at it, . . .
Now for the surprise.
I'm inviting you . . .
With your permission, I'd like to . . .
Are we out of our minds to make you an
    offer like this?

So there you have it.
So if you want to enjoy . . .
No wonder . . .
That's why . . .
What's more, . . .
Most important, . . .
Best of all, . . .
Last but not least, . . .
So remember . . .
So don't forget . . .
And that's what _____ is all about.
We've saved the best for last.

ALL-PURPOSE GRABBERS

win	proven	solution
free	tested	breakthrough
bonus	safe	guarantee
value	successful	easy
offer	powerful	simple/simply
sale	amazing	instantly
save/savings	valuable	less
bargain	don't	lowest
discount	ever	nothing
now	never	Our loss is your gain!
you/your/yours	always	Now you too can . . .
I	please	Now for the first time . . .
we	start	By popular demand
only	stop	This is your last chance to . . .
more	avoid	Hurry in for these . . .
most	solve	Don't miss . . .
big/biggest	make	Good news!
unlimited	eliminate	It's true!
extra	enjoy	Fact:
plus	get	Amazing _____ breakthrough!
complete	order	Sneak preview!
totally	hurry	New low price!
absolutely	today	Ask for your free _____.
best	new	_____ reasons you should buy . . .
best-selling	latest	Check these great features:
top-rated	exclusive	Here's what you get:
famous	secret	The first . . .
original	tip	The only . . .
genuine	answer	At last!

PART 2

DESCRIPTIONS AND BENEFITS

CONVEYING THE VALUE OF YOUR PRODUCT OR SERVICE

APPEALING

irresistible
special
delightful
wonderful
marvelous
enchanting
magical
charming
engaging
winning
captivating
beguiling
alluring
fetching
inviting
bewitching
sparkling
zesty
yummy
luscious
hearty
fresh
lovely
pleasing
pleasant
winsome

lovable
huggable
cuddly
adorable
cute
cozy
congenial
enthralling
exquisite
perfect
picture-perfect
picturesque
decorative
colorful
cheerful
cheery
sunny
vibrant
vivid
entertaining
amusing
joyous
satisfying
moving
poignant
evocative

memorable
unforgettable
You'll never forget . . .
never to be forgotten
You'll love . . .
You'll fall in love with . . .
You'll enjoy . . .
Experience the wonder of . . .
brightens your . . .
just the right touch of . . .
a winning combination of . . .
the allure of . . .
a gem
a joy
pure enjoyment
an unexpected pleasure
. . . beckons

For further inspiration, see:
Fabulous
Fun/Cheerful
Good-Looking
Pleasure/Satisfaction
Romantic
Sexy
Stylish

AUTHENTIC

true
actual
real
genuine
the genuine article
original
the original _____
original formula
original recipe
from an old family recipe
the way _____ used to make it
the first _____
the one and only
honest
honest-to-goodness
legitimate
valid
convincing
certified
backed by . . .
proven
time-proven
tested
time-tested
our reptuation for . . .
authenticity
faithful to . . .
realistic

real-life
true-life
true-to-life
not a reproduction
an exact replica
meticulously reproduced
indistinguishable from the original
faithful to . . .
faithful in every detail
unadulterated
inimitable
unmistakable
the one and only
the _____ of record
We created . . .
We invented . . .
We pioneered . . .
We originated . . .
We're the originators of . . .
We're the ones who . . .
We were the first to . . .
We were there at the beginning.
We started it all.

For further inspiration, see:
Experienced/Expert
Honest
Reliable

BELONGING/ MEMBERSHIP

join
enter
meet
mingle
share
associate (v.)/associates (n.)
members
friends
companions
buddies
colleagues
peers
allies
partners
like-minded people
your link with . . .
your ticket to . . .
your passport to . . .
Sign up for . . .
Connect with . . .
Stay connected with . . .
Hook up with . . .
Rub elbows with . . .
Socialize with . . .
Network with . . .
Make new friends . . .
Make valuable contacts . . .
Build strategic alliances . . .
Meet the movers and shakers . . .

Meet kindred spirits . . .
Feel the warmth of . . .
Participate in . . .
Be a part of . . .
Take part in . . .
Get into . . .
Stay engaged . . .
Exchange ideas with . . .
Swap stories with . . .
Stay in the loop . . .
VIP membership
gold membership
As a member of _____, you'll . . .
As a member in good standing, . . .
You'll join the ranks of . . .
You'll join a very select group.
You'll be in on . . .
You'll be welcomed into . . .
You'll be privy to . . .
You'll enjoy these special privileges:
We'll treat you to these special perks:
You'll join thousands of other _____s
people who share your interest in _____
the benefits of membership
the privileges of membership
the many satisfactions of membership

For further inspiration, see:
Distinguished/Status

BIG / MANY

large

huge

enormous

gigantic

giant

tremendous

spectacular

monumental

massive

mammoth

jumbo

immense

oversized

sizable

generously proportioned

man-sized

king-size

whopping

monster

titanic

colossal

gargantuan

towering

lofty

soaring

super

grand

great

mega_____

giga_____

vast

substantial

ample

ample room for . . .

roomy

spacious

voluminous

expansive

full-cut

large-scale

a large canvas

of epic proportion

the biggest

the mother of all _____s

heavyweight

weighty

hefty

husky

stout

burly

wall-to-wall _____

a _____ bonanza

panoramic scope

unlimited

limitless

without limits

countless

numerous

extensive
boundless
plentiful
abundant
an abundance of . . .
a feast of . . .
a gold mine of . . .
a treasure trove of . . .
a host of . . .
a wealth of . . .
a staggering array of . . .
a wide range of . . .
a vast collection of . . .
a huge selection of . . .
a sweeping variety of . . .
an endless source of . . .
a bottomless supply of . . .
a profusion of . . .
a multitude of . . .
mountains of . . .
a medley of . . .
packed with . . .
filled with . . .
loaded with . . .
crammed with . . .
chock full of . . .

abounds with . . .
_____ galore!
lavishly . . .
profusely . . .
multiple . . .
rich diversity
to the max
. . . and we don't stop there!
Take your pick:
You get all this:
. . . and lots more!
Maximize your _____.
Grow your _____.
Expand your _____.
Broaden your _____.
Increase your _____.
Build your _____.
Multiply your _____.
Extend your _____.
Boost your _____.

For further inspiration, see:
Choice/Control
Complete/Thorough
Powerful

CHOICE/CONTROL

options
alternatives
selection
components
modular
flexibility
freedom
compare
choose
pick
select
assemble
_____ on demand
. . . to your specifications
whichever _____ you prefer
whatever your preference
whatever your pleasure
whenever it's convenient for you
gives you the power to . . .
puts you in charge
Take charge of . . .
puts you at the controls
Take control of . . .

You're in control.
You have total control of . . .
You control the _____.
You direct the _____.
You guide the _____.
You choose the _____.
You have a choice of . . .
The choice is yours:
Choose from . . .
Select from . . .
Customize it . . .
customizable
a wide range of customizing options
Adapt it to your specific needs.
Fine-tune your _____.
Create a _____ that's the perfect
   reflection of *you*.
No other _____ offers this much
   flexibility.
Nobody offers you more . . .
more _____ than any other _____
more _____ to choose from than
   any other _____

so many _____ to choose from
_____ styles to choose from
our vast selection of . . .
our huge inventory of . . .
our full line of . . .
our extensive repertoire of . . .
This is just a partial list of . . .
They're all here:
Keep just the ones you want.
Order as many or as few as
   you like.
Take your pick . . .
You decide . . .
Do it your way.
You're totally free to . . .
Think of the possibilities.
We can handle any request.
You name it, we've got it.

For further inspiration, see:
Big/Many
Convenient
Security/Peace of Mind

COMFORTABLE

soothing
snug
comfy
roomy
airy
cheerful
peaceful
down-home
casual
country casual
informal
relaxed
relaxing
restful
unhurried
at ease
a haven of . . .
tranquil
serene
placid
hospitable
congenial
friendly
unassuming
Snuggle up with . . .
Cuddle up with . . .
cuddly
cushiony
plush

soft
glove-soft
whisper-soft
baby-soft
smooth as silk
satiny
velvety
downy
feathery
fleecy
cottony
fuzzy
furry
billowy
slouchy
stretchy
supple
freedom of movement
cut full for extra comfort
loose-fitting
easy-fitting
easy-to-wear
superb fit
snug-fitting
firm support
ergonomically designed
just the way you like it
It breathes.
breathable

Bask in . . .
Luxuriate in . . .
bathes you in . . .
surrounds you with . . .
envelops you in . . .
like floating on a puffy cloud
cool comfort
cool as a summer breeze
toasty-warm
cool in summer, warm in winter
Stay warm and dry . . .
Stay cool and dry . . .
Get relief from . . .
Get comfortable with . . .
long on comfort
one of life's little comforts
the comforts of home
the latest in comfort
all-day comfort
the ultimate in comfort
for unsurpassed comfort
You won't know you're
    wearing it.
It already feels broken-in.
It just feels right.

For further inspiration, see:
Appealing
Security/Peace of Mind

COMPETITIVE

feisty
gutsy
scrappy
hungry
lean-and-mean
hard-driving
hard-hitting
high-energy
intense
smart
shrewd
sharp
astute
savvy
enterprising
proactive
assertive
aggressive
in-your-face
potent
bold
daring
innovative

cutting-edge
creative
energetic
dynamic
forceful
tough
tough-as-nails
masterful
commanding
a power player
point for point
pound for pound
goes the distance
never lets up
outperforms
blows away the competition
consistently outperforms the
    competition
guerrilla tactics
kick-ass competitors
seasoned warriors
our winning team
the _____ challenge

We challenge . . .
We pursue . . .
We're not afraid to . . .
We fight for your . . .
We go head-to-head with . . .
We take on the big boys . . .
We're passionate about winning.
We'll match our _____ against . . .
We've rewritten the rules . . .
We've reinvented . . .
We've caught the competition
    napping.
We consistently beat them at
    their own game.
Just let them try to beat our _____.
No other _____ comes close.

For further inspiration, see:
Results/Performance
Superior
**Enhancing Your Company's
    Image (Part 4)**
Knocking the Competition (Part 4)

COMPLETE/THOROUGH

comprehensive
in-depth
extensive
unlimited
limitless
all-inclusive
all _____ included
everything you need
everything you've always wanted
    in a _____
everything you've always wanted
    to know about _____
everything from _____ to _____
A to Z
more _____ than any other _____
a _____ and a _____ in one
the most complete _____ you
    can buy
the only _____ you'll ever need
your complete _____
a complete package

complete in one package
all in one place
. . . in one convenient source
everything you need in one box
It's all here!
They're all here:
outfitted with . . .
complete with . . .
all the features you'd expect
all the right ingredients
100% of the _____ you need
the all-in-one _____
your all-in-one _____
the ultimate _____
the total _____
the sum total of . . .
an endless source of . . .
an extensive repertoire of . . .
a bottomless reservoir of . . .
jam-packed with . . .
totally packed

tremendous scope
panoramic
sweeping
encyclopedic
full-length
uncut
unexpurgated
uncensored
unedited
unabridged
definitive
exhaustive
meticulously prepared
scrupulously researched
We've taken great pains to . . .
doesn't stop with _____

For further inspiration, see:
Big/Many
Choice/Control
Superior

CONVENIENT

handy

versatile

practical

facilitates

simplifies

clarifies

right at your fingertips

within easy reach

easily accessible

fast, easy access

gives you instant access to . . .

time-saving

efficient

built for efficiency

practically runs itself

quick reference

instant reference

a single source

all in one place

no more endless searching

no more rummaging

no more standing in line

no more waiting

no more headaches

Never again will you have to . . .

Say goodbye to . . .

without the hassle of . . .

combines the best features of . . .

a _____ and a _____ in one

a marriage of _____ and _____

mobile

mobility

ultra-mobile

for added mobility

conveniently portable

take it anywhere

ready to go

go-anywhere convenience

travels anywhere

portable enough to go anywhere

the perfect traveling companion

goes wherever you go

stay connected anywhere

at home or in the office

in the office or on the road

ideal for road warriors

in your own home

in the privacy of your home

brings _____ right into your living room

_____ from anywhere in your house

_____ from your living room sofa

armchair shopping

fits your schedule

at your own convenience

pushbutton convenience

with the flick of a switch

automatic

automatically

automates your _____
strategically located
just a short stroll from . . .
located right in the heart of . . .
You won't have to shop around.
one-stop shopping
direct to you
delivered to your doorstep
a time-saver
streamlines your _____
eliminates the need for . . .
intelligently designed to . . .
flexible design
conveniently flexible
_____ on demand
ready to use
ready for installation
installs in seconds
installs in minutes
comes fully assembled
transports easily
ships flat
easy storage
easy to assemble
modular
detachable
collapsible
stackable
expandable
adjustable
adaptable

reusable
refillable
disposable
maneuverable
machine-washable
just the right size for . . .
one size fits all
compatible with any _____
interchangeable
adapts to your lifestyle
for any occasion
whenever you want it
wherever and whenever
the _____ you need, whenever you need it
It's there when you need it.
whenever you feel like . . .
at your own pace
takes the work out of . . .
makes _____ easier than ever
maintenance-free
needs little or no maintenance
self-cleaning
never needs polishing
never needs replacing
Use once and toss.

For further inspiration, see:
Choice/Control
Easy
Service/Help
Useful/Practical

DISTINGUISHED / STATUS

important
significant
prize-winning
prestigious
elite
major
premier
outstanding
accomplished
eminent
prominent
noted
notable
noteworthy
famous
celebrated
honored
respected
esteemed
acclaimed
renowned
illustrious
legendary
revered
exalted
venerated
privileged
noble
aristocratic

well-bred
patrician
stately
dignified
imposing
grand
commanding
influential
dominant
authoritative
selective
highly selective
discriminating
private
exclusive
among the most exclusive
world-class
top-ranked
top-ranking
high-ranking
highest-ranking
highly regarded
held in high regard
the absolute . . .
an icon
a landmark
the nation's leading _____
the nation's most distinguished _____
the nation's most respected _____

the nation's most influential _____
the Harvard of _____
a *Who's Who* of _____
the greatest
the best
the foremost
the most talked about
the most imitated
used by Fortune 500 companies
used by top executives
the choice of today's movers and shakers
the choice of connoisseurs
the preferred _____
preferred by people who make a difference
a _____ of obvious distinction
has won accolades
has won the respect of . . .
has played a major role in . . .
the one and only . . .
prestige
cachet
class
rank
sought-after
must-have
strictly upscale
found only in museums and distinguished
   private collections
commissioned exclusively for _____
a symbol of . . .
an emblem of . . .
identifies you as . . .

reflects your position
confers upon its owner . . .
connects you with . . .
automatically entitles you to . . .
all the amenities
VIP treatment
gives you an insider's grasp of . . .
takes you behind closed doors
a privileged glimpse
. . . of the rich and famous
where today's power brokers call the shots
where today's movers and shakers are congregating
the value of a _____ address
a prestigious address
recognized by discriminating _____s everywhere
the discriminating few
the discerning few
Until now, only a fortunate few have been
   able to . . .
our educated, well-informed listeners/members/
   readers/viewers/clients
Come up to _____.
Enjoy the view from the top.
Isn't it time you treated yourself to _____?

For further inspiration, see:
Belonging/Membership
Luxurious
Sophisticated/Smart
Superior
Flattering the Reader (Section 4)
Using Demographics to Impress (Part 4)

DURABLE / SOLID

firm
hard
strong
resilient
sturdy
hefty
heavyweight
rugged
brawny
beefy
tough
hardy
robust
well-built
high-impact
impact-resistant
rock-solid
structurally solid
ballistic
armored
reinforced
seamless
one-piece construction

rugged construction
long-lasting
long-wearing
lasts for years
lasts a lifetime
built to last
ruggedly built
heavy-duty
high-performance
virtually indestructible
practically bulletproof
unbreakable
shatterproof
waterproof
watertight
water-repellent
colorfast
resists fading
stain-resistant
heat-resistant
microwave-safe
oven-safe
scuff-proof

rust-resistant
corrosion-free
tamper-proof
ironclad
can take a beating
won't ever wear out
stands up to . . .
impervious to . . .
tough enough to . . .
shrugs off _____
scoffs at _____
built to withstand the elements
takes the hard knocks
designed for a lifetime of
    daily use
the last _____ you'll ever need
    to buy

For further inspiration, see:
Luxurious
Reliable
Results/Performance

EASY

effortless/effortlessly
intuitive
uncomplicated
straightforward
automatic
foolproof
step-by-step
clear
user-friendly
fast
quick
quick and easy
instant _____
at a glance
easy to follow
easy to understand
simplified
amazingly simple
elegantly simple
clearly and simply explained
great for beginners
a crash course in _____
You don't have to be an expert.
even if you're a novice
takes the mystique out of . . .
takes the work out of . . .
It's that simple!
It's a snap . . .
It's a cinch . . .

It couldn't be easier.
_____ has never been easier.
It's never been easier to . . .
Discover how easy it is to . . .
All you do is . . .
in no time at all
no fussing
no headaches
no more struggling with . . .
no tedious _____
no sweat
piece of cake
smooth sailing
safe and simple
child's play
facilitates
clarifies
simplifies
simplicity itself
the easy way
_____ made easy
easier than ever before
clearly written
written in plain English
fast-reading
easy to understand
easy to use
a streamlined approach
a simplified approach

jargon-free
coasting all the way
with the flick of a switch
with the touch of a button
. . . with incredible ease
one-step _____
all in one easy step
no assembly required
no _____ required
accessible
fast, easy access
so advanced, it's actually simple
capability without complexity
one touch and it . . .
easy to assemble
installs in minutes
ready to use
ready to go
practically runs itself
trouble-free
maintenance-free
little or no maintenance
low-maintenance
easy-care
no pampering required
_____ just got easier.

For further inspiration, see:
Convenient

EXCITING/STIMULATING

entertaining
fun
lively
vibrant
colorful
vivid
imaginative
spontaneous
exhilarating
thrilling
pulse-pounding
spellbinding
mesmerizing
electrifying
jaw-dropping
stunning
startling
shocking
surprising
sensational
spectacular
dramatic
provocative
thought-provoking
intelligent
literate
incisive
fascinating
gripping

intriguing
absorbing
engrossing
riveting
compelling
challenging
inspiring
rousing
stirring
alluring
enticing
titillating
tantalizing
sizzling
hot
sexy
spicy
racy
heady
giddy
sassy
edgy
baddest
reckless
wild
delirious
wired
juiced
daring

unreal
delicious
outrageous
electrifying
terrifying
explosive
amazing
awesome
overwhelming
earthshaking
ultimate
extreme _____
outlaw _____
killer _____
_____ rocks!
Wow!
a knockout
off the charts
slam-dunk
in the zone
never lets up
the thrill of _____
an adventure in _____
sweeps you along
catapults you
energizes you
blasts you
startles you
thrills you

shocks you
terrifies you
revives you
tantalizes you
challenges you
tickles the mind
stirs your emotions
rouses your senses
a dazzling display of . . .

the unexpected thrill of . . .
Thrill to the . . .
Experience the . . .
Feel the energy . . .
Catch the excitement . . .
Fasten your seatbelt
a roller coaster ride never to
   be forgotten
takes _____ to the next level

For further inspiration, see:
Appealing
Fabulous
Fun/Cheerful
Pleasure/Satisfaction
Powerful
Sexy

EXPERIENCED / EXPERT

talented

qualified

accomplished

skilled

trained

seasoned

proficient

capable

gifted

ingenious

authoritative

exacting

professional

veteran

savvy

ace

recognized

influential

honored

prize-winning

our award-winning staff

our professional staff

our trained staff

our expert staff

our team of experts

a crack team of . . .

We're professionals.

We're pros.

developed in coordination with leading _____

. . . have combined their talents

. . . have pooled their expertise

professional expertise

field-proven

our proven track record

authority

the foremost authority

We're the original _____ .

for over _____ years

since [date]

pioneers in . . .

solid experience

talent for . . .

flair for . . .

mastery of . . .

masters at . . .

the artistry of . . .

the wizardry of . . .

craftsmanship

meticulously crafted

expertly engineered

endowed with . . .

well versed in . . .

virtuoso

genius for . . .

ingenuity

talent and imagination

the stamp of creativity

our vision

We've got the right stuff.
We've got the talent.
We're dedicated to . . .
We have hands-on experience with . . .
We're thoroughly familiar with . . .
We're totally obsessed with . . .
We advise . . .
We evaluate . . .
We solve . . .
We question . . .
We create . . .
We invented . . .
We developed . . .
We pioneered the . . .
We're the ones who . . .
We had the foresight to . . .
We've shaped the growth of . . .
competence
imagination
finesse
proficiency
professionalism
held in high regard by . . .
our exacting standards
our standards of excellence

our commitment to excellence
America's leading _____
_____'s most respected _____
_____'s #1 _____
Your _____ experts.
top-drawer talent
tops in our field
top credentials
the best in the businesss
_____ is what we do best.
_____ is what we've always done better than
   anyone else.
_____ is our business.
There's simply no substitute for _____.
Don't just take our word for it.
Put us to the test.

For further inspiration, see:
Reliable
Results/Performance
Service/Help
Superior
Enhancing Your Company's Image (Part 4)
Knocking the Competition (Part 4)

FABULOUS

great
magnificent
dazzling
splendid
breathtaking
astonishing
sublime
spectacular
incredible
remarkable
terrific
amazing
sensational
sumptuous
opulent
majestic
elegant
fantastic
cool
hot
sizzling
smokin'
awesome
awe-inspiring
striking
earthshaking
monumental
wonderful

wondrous
marvelous
miraculous
glorious
exalted
superb
unsurpassed
unparalleled
unprecedented
unforgettable
incomparable
the pinnacle of . . .
tops
a towering achievement
a monument to . . .
a masterpiece
stunning
sparkling
glittering
exquisite
a treasure
a marvel
a joy
pure joy
sheer bliss
a celebration of . . .
an extravaganza
a once-in-a-lifetime spectacle

You've never seen anything
   like _____.
never before
must be seen to be believed
the _____ you've been waiting for
the kind of _____ you've only
   dreamed about
A _____'s dream!
undreamed of
the magic of _____
the miracle of _____
defies description
flat-out _____
killer _____
_____ rules!
one hell of a _____
takes no prisoners
will amaze you
off the charts
never to be forgotten

For further inspiration, see:
Exciting/Stimulating
Fun/Cheerful
Powerful
Sensory Qualities
Superior

FAST

instant
immediate
swift
speedy
fast-paced
punctual
prompt
quick
rapid
brisk
accelerated
express
hustling
without delay
A.S.A.P.
full throttle
high-velocity
in a flash
in nanoseconds
in seconds
in minutes
in a couple of hours
a same-day solution
in days

days instead of weeks
in a matter of weeks
in a fraction of the time it takes
   to . . .
in no time at all
at the speed of light
at the speed of sound
speeds along
zips along
tears along
dashes
sprints
scoots
smokes
zooms
plunges
soars
flies
cruises
outpaces
overtakes
whizzes past
races ahead
races into the lead

whoosh!
vroooom!
works immediately
instantly
goes to work in seconds
fast-acting
fast results
hard-driving
expedites
facilitates
quick turnaround
in half the time
faster than you ever thought
   possible
free same-day installation
gets you up and running in
   minutes

For further inspiration, see:
Convenient
Easy
Powerful
Results/Performance
Timely

FRESH / WHOLESOME

light (lite)
airy
sparkling
clean
clear
pure
pristine
virgin
mild
soothing
refreshing
hearty
bracing
rejuvenating
invigorating
healthful
healthy
health-giving
a tonic for . . .
sealed-in freshness
fragrant
floral

a bouquet of . . .
a breath of . . .
natural
all-natural
whole _____
homemade
homespun
down-home
old-fashioned goodness
fresh from the oven
oven-fresh
sunshine fresh
whiter-than-white
crystal-clear
immaculate
revives your . . .
will renew your . . .
makes you feel brand-new
makes you feel good from top
    to bottom
arrive refreshed
freshen up

the way nature made it
the way nature intended
natural goodness
nothing artificial
nothing added
no additives
organically grown
untainted by . . .
from the earth
the earth's finest . . .
clean and fresh
cool and refreshing
cool and crisp
cool comfort

For further inspiration, see:
Appealing
Comfortable
Healthful
Plain/Natural
Sensory Qualities

FUN / CHEERFUL

amusing/amusement
hilarious/hilarity
entertaining/entertainment
diverting/diversion
merry/merriment
whimsical/whimsy
mirthful/mirth
blissful/bliss
lighthearted
joyous/joy
cheery
rollicking
festive
hearty
jolly
jubilant
giddy
dizzy
sunny
carefree
happy
breezy
funny/droll
playful
perky
convivial
feel-good
wild
electrifying

delirious
madcap
a romp
a caper
a lark
a hoot
a riot
a joyride
an adventure
a celebration
a gala _____
a pleasure feast
an extravaganza
escapades
antics
revels/revelry
festivities
good times
glee
gaiety
recreation
just for kicks
just for laughs
laugh-a-minute
hours/years of fun
frolic
carouse
make merry
Indulge yourself.

Revel in . . .
Enjoy!
Enjoy your favorite . . .
whoop it up
laugh
giggle
chuckle
belly laughs
knee-slapping
a laugh riot
a screwball comedy
. . . with total abandon
The fun begins with _____.
Let yourself go.
Get away . . .
Leave your headaches behind.
De-stress yourself.
takes the chore out of _____.
makes your day
brightens your spirits
gives you a lift
boosts your mood
tickles you

For further inspiration, see:
Exciting/Stimulating
Pleasure/Satisfaction

GIFT

a handsome gift
a thoughtful gift
a tasteful gift
a memorable gift
a useful and distinctive gift
a gift that will be used and
  appreciated
a gift that will always be
  remembered
Everyone loves . . .
the perfect gift for . . .
an ideal gift for . . .
for those special people on
  your list
for those deserving people
for the VIPs in your life
for a special friend or relative
for your valued colleagues,
  clients, and customers
perfect for _____ buffs
will delight connoisseurs of _____
for every devotee of _____
for every _____ aficionado
for your holiday gift-giving needs

a gift that keeps on giving
the gift of beauty
the gift of success
the gift of love
a one-of-a-kind gift
hard-to-find gifts
"can't-miss" items
as handsome as it is functional
elegant yet practical
giftworthy
impeccably correct
always tasteful and correct
elegantly wrapped
makes an eye-popping
  presentation
will be readily used and
  appreciated
won't sit on the shelf
won't go back in the box
Think of the special bond you'll
  create when you give . . .
Give your children a head start . . .
Give your family a fitting
  legacy . . .

. . . will benefit them as long as
  they live.
brimming with gift ideas
You won't have to look beyond
  this catalog/brochure/site.
Do your gift shopping at home.
no more last-minute treks
  through the mall
our gift to you
especially for you
Take it—it's yours!
yours to keep
bonus
prize
premium
giveaway
donation
contribution

For further inspiration, see:
Free/Prize (Part 1)
Luxurious
Suitable

GOOD-LOOKING

lovely
beautiful
attractive
striking
handsome
head-turning
eye-catching
smart-looking
fine-looking
great-looking
gorgeous
splendid
stunning
dazzling
breathtaking
ravishing
smashing
shimmering
glittering
sparkling
glowing
luminous
radiant
vibrant
elegant
magnificent
resplendent
impeccable
flawless

perfect
exquisite
dainty
pretty
ethereal
gossamer
graceful
streamlined
neat
trim
sleek
contoured
shapely
alluring
seductive
sensuous
sexy
charming
appealing
fetching
enticing
enchanting
captivating
winning
flattering
luscious
delicious
delectable
knockout

glamorous
big on looks
long on looks
a head-turner
to die for
killer _____
outrageous
awesome
full-bodied
voluptuous
long and lean
slim and sultry
clean lines
elegant lines
sits nicely
well-proportioned
perfectly proportioned
smartly designed
artfully designed
designed to flatter
très belle
très jolie
look your best
the beauty is in the . . .
timeless beauty
enduring beauty
world-class beauty
fragile beauty
haunting beauty

rare beauty
unforgettable beauty
a vision of . . .
visual poetry
a visual explosion
a visual treat
a visual delight
a visual feast
a feast for the eyes
eye candy
eye-pleasing
easy on the eyes
handsomely fashioned

devastatingly handsome
impeccably handsome
ruggedly handsome
rakish
macho
dashing
sporty
dapper
distinguished
distinctive
aristocratic
antiqued
burnished

lustrous
gleaming
glossy
bronzed
golden
silvery
crystalline
gemlike

For further inspiration, see:
Appealing
Sexy

HEALTHFUL

low-fat
low-calorie
low-sugar
high-fiber
nutritious
fortifying
invigorating
rejuvenating
refreshing
soothing
healing
natural
all-natural
natural goodness
natural remedy
nothing artificial
nothing added
no additives
It's not a pill.
herbal
homeopathic
organic
organically grown

untainted by . . .
safe and effective
safer and more effective than
    "fad" diets
no side effects
clinically tested
clinically proven
FDA-approved
protects your immune
    system
raises your metabolism
lowers your blood pressure
    without drugs
banishes pain
eases tension
relieves stress
instant stress relief
stressbusting
deep relaxation
relaxes your _____
restores your _____
fast relief from _____
promotes fast healing

stimulates your body's own
    healing process
provides the essential nutrients
    your body needs to . . .
replaces flab with muscle
melts away those extra pounds
boosts your endurance
boosts your energy level
helps restore your vitality
helps you recover from . . .
helps you reach your ideal
    weight
helps you lose as much or as
    little weight as you want
helps revive your sex drive
helps you look and feel years
    younger
makes you feel good all over

For further inspiration, see:
Fresh/Wholesome
Plain/Natural
Self-Improvement

HONEST

truthful
candid
frank
reliable
straightforward
straight-shooting
no-nonsense
evenhanded
unbiased
fair-minded
outspoken
forthright
up-front
blunt
gutsy
feisty
opinionated
provocative
revealing
uninhibited
eye-opening
no-holds-barred
hard-hitting
point-blank

tough
unequivocal
sincere
open
direct
genuine
authentic
reputable
reliable
steadfast
stalwart
staunch
ethical
incorruptible
principled
believable
integrity
character
straight talk about . . .
the plain truth
the honest truth
the truth about _____
plain English
jargon-free

cold hard facts
just the facts
You get the facts . . .
We offer proof.
We explode the myths about . . .
We probe . . .
We uncover . . .
We unmask . . .
We don't pull punches.
We strip away the . . .
an exposé of . . .
a critical eye
honest-to-goodness
Let's be honest about . . .
a reputation for honesty
a name you can trust

For further inspiration, see:
Authentic
Plain/Natural
Reliable
Enhancing Your Company's
   Image (Part 4)

IMPROVED

changed
upgraded
updated
transformed
expanded
enriched
enhanced
modified
refurbished
remodeled
redesigned
restored
reformed
revolutionized
renewed
revived
rejuvenated
revamped
reorganized
restructured
re-created
refined
beautified
spruced up

embellished
perfected
a new look
new design
new refinements
newly redesigned
newly revised
newly improved
now improved
newly upgraded
the best yet
better than ever
bigger and better than ever
more _____ than ever
the first real improvement
    in _____ since . . .
There's more to like than
    ever before.
a time to grow and change
now with more _____
increased _____
great new _____
The best just got better.
Now you get . . .

We've given _____ a facelift.
more than a facelift
We've bettered . . .
We've beaten . . .
We've built . . .
We've redesigned . . .
We've transformed .. .
We've revolutionized . . .
We've changed the rules . . .
a change for the better
a new image
a renaissance
a revolution in the making
an about-face
If you haven't tried _____ lately,
    you're in for a surprise.
Put the new features to work
    right now.
We're growing to serve you
    better.
Of course, we'll continue to . . .

For further inspiration, see:
New/Advanced

INDISPENSABLE

essential
important
significant
valuable
invaluable
incalculable
vital
crucial
critical
urgent
consequential
fundamental
basic
imperative
obligatory
a *must*
a *must-have* item
a necessity
much-needed
the bible of . . .
the _____ no home should be without
a _____ you simply can't afford to miss
a _____ you can't get along without
an indispensable tool
the foundation of any _____
a basic element of any _____

standard equipment
an essential ingredient
an essential resource
a vital link
a prerequisite
the primary . . .
the chief . . .
the principal . . .
the foundation of . . .
the heart of . . .
the key to . . .
the core of . . .
the hub of . . .
the nerve center of . . .
the most widely used _____
always in demand
Don't _____ without it!
You'll wonder how you ever got along without it.
Don't you think you need _____ ?
the basis of any good _____

For further inspiration, see:
Reliable
Superior
Useful/Practical
Valuable

INFORMATIVE

instructive
educational
incisive
illuminating
enlightening
eye-opening
mind-opening
detailed
in-depth
authoritative
influential
newsy
keeps you in touch with . . .
keeps you current with . . .
keeps you informed
. . . while it informs
expands your knowledge
changes your perceptions
stirs the imagination
will familiarize you with . . .
gives you an insider's grasp of . . .
arms you with vital insights
stretches your mind
takes the guesswork out of . . .
takes the mystery out of . . .
unlocks the secrets of . . .

reveals the _____ behind
    the _____
takes you behind closed doors
tells all
dishes the dirt
gives you access to . . .
helps you keep pace with . . .
lets you in on everything that's
    happening
keeps you ahead of the game
gives you the hard facts
helps you separate fact from
    fiction
gives you the facts you need to
    make important decisions
opens up new channels of
    information
satisfies your need to know
gives you new insight
brings you fresh perspectives
the answers you've always
    wanted
the answers to these and
    hundreds of other questions
everything you always wanted
    to know about _____

everything you need to know
    about _____
instant feedback
valuable input
hard-won wisdom
step-by-step techniques
little-known techniques
expert advice
useful advice
lucid analysis
inside information
a wealth of information
information-packed
great ideas for . . .
Stay in the loop . . .
Stay abreast of . . .
Get the latest scoop on . . .
We bring it all into focus
    for you.

For further inspiration, see:
Complete/Thorough
Exciting/Stimulating
Honest
Self-Improvement
Service/Help

LUXURIOUS

rich
plush
ornate
opulent
posh
lush
swank
extravagant
lavish
deluxe
luxe
sumptuous
precious
embellished
glittering
gemlike
the glint of gold
gilt-edged
glamorous
splendid
superb
regal
palatial
grand
stately
imposing
distinctive
magnificent
first-class

upscale
high-end
refined
elegant
classic
heirloom-quality
museum-quality
masterpiece
craftsmanship
luxuriously handcrafted
elegantly handcrafted
handmade
intricate detailing
limited edition
rare
fancy
exquisite
valuable
invaluable
treasured
superior
elite
sinfully rich
delightfully decadent
elegantly appointed
specially commissioned
flagrantly expensive, and worth
    every penny
worth the expense

a _____ of obvious distinction
a _____ you'll be proud to own
an affordable luxury
an affordable extravagance
extravagant touches
_____ signifies quality
Go in style.
Pamper yourself.
charm and grandeur
unrestrained luxury
the ultimate in luxury
beautiful accoutrements
becomes more precious with time
quality that suits your style
wraps you in glamour
always in perfect taste
spoils you for anything else
caters to the discriminating few
only the finest
all the amenities
for those who demand excellence
where excellence is a tradition

For further inspiration, see:
Distinguished/Status
Made
Stylish
Superior
Justifying a High Price (Part 4)

MADE

created
formulated
developed
manufactured
built
constructed
assembled
put together
engineered
produced
fashioned
formed
shaped
hewn
forged
molded
conceived
designed
gathered from . . .
fabricated
tooled
precision-made
precision-engineered
precision-tooled

custom-built
custom-manufactured
custom-fitted
custom-designed
handcrafted
handmade
hand-tooled
hand-rubbed
hand-burnished
hand-colored
hand-dyed
hand-sewn
made the old-fashioned way
crafted by skilled artisans
shaped by skilled hands
re-created
reproduced
faithfully crafted
finely crafted
lovingly crafted
individually crafted
meticulously handcrafted
luxuriously handcrafted
deftly designed

solidly built
classically styled
developed in coordination
   with leading _____
made to our high standards
made to our exacting
   specifications
built to last
built for the ages
masterfully sculpted
masters of their craft
timeless craftsmanship
Old World craftsmanship
flawless craftsmanship
precision craftsmanship
intricate detailing
attention to detail
hallmarks of . . .
a legacy of . . .

For further inspiration, see:
Luxurious
New/Advanced
Durable/Solid

MONEY-MAKING

money-making opportunity
a golden opportunity
the opportunity of a lifetime
Make money the easy way.
Build wealth the easy way.
We'll show you the money.
Double your earnings!
How rich people get that way.
_____ your way to wealth!
Make your first million in _____.
Do you sincerely want to make
   a million?
Dozens of money-making
   opportunities!
Turn your _____ into gold!
Profit from . . .
Cash in on . . .
Turn your free time into profits.
Earn a comfortable living without
   the hassle of a 9-to-5 job.
. . . will pay big dividends.
the fast track to wealth
undreamed-of riches
dynamic growth potential
pays off
the payoff
high yields
tax-free earnings
Watch your money grow.

Create interest.
Build your nest egg.
growth potential
multiplies your investment
Double your investment . . .
Protect your investment.
a smart investment
a wise investment
where today's smart money is
   being invested
a small investment that will repay
   itself many times over
the return on your investment . . .
unlimited earnings
top dollar
top salary
megabucks
money in the bank
good as gold
a three-step formula that
   guarantees success
my personal formula for wealth
guaranteed formula
Now get *paid* for . . .
Make a fortune in _____!
Earn a residual income from . . .
Create a lifetime income stream . . .
Run a successful _____ business
   in your spare time.

Earn $_____ a month in your
   spare time!
Earn up to $_____ your first year!
How much you earn is up to you.
Rack up profits.
generates profits
easy profits
profit leaders
profitable
new profit sources
Reach profitable new markets.
Boost productivity and profits.
high turnover
cold cash
hot sellers
perennial best-sellers
They sell themselves!
sizzling sales
revenue stream
Your commissions will multiply.
Watch your profits soar!
guaranteed to boost sales
Over _____ million sold!
a hot item
keeps on selling

For further inspiration, see:
Money-Saving
Self-Improvement

MONEY-SAVING

inexpensive
affordable
economical
thrifty
low-cost
low-priced
value-priced
budget-priced
discount-priced
bargain-priced
invitingly priced
sale-priced
priced to sell
rock-bottom prices
popular prices
unheard-of low prices
direct-to-you prices
affordably priced
surprisingly affordable
super-affordable
at a price you can afford
a fantastic bargain
dramatic savings
huge savings
a truckload of savings
hot deals
at a fraction of the cost
at a fraction of the original price
only $_____

a $_____ value—now only $_____
only $_____ with mail-in rebate
an unbeatable value
guaranteed lowest prices
lowest prices allowed by law
marked down
prices slashed
huge discounts
below wholesale
extra savings
remarkable cash savings
extra value
big value
a smart buy
a best buy
a best bet
the best deal in town
your money's worth
more for your money
pays for itself
fits your budget
easy on your budget
_____ easy payments
saves you time and money
the best _____ for your money
first-class _____ at no-frills prices
designer quality at mass-market prices
maximum value at minimum cost
Imagine being able to get a _____ for only $_____.

And you thought you couldn't afford _____!
Finally, a _____ you can afford.
Why pay retail for _____?
Compare our prices with . . .
You won't believe this price!
Just $_____ covers it all.
Anywhere else you could expect to pay up to
    $_____ for . . .
Until now you would have had to pay up to
    $_____ for . ..
Save a bundle on _____.
_____ minutes of your time could save you _____%.
You save because . . .
We've eliminated the middleman.
No middleman!
Our loss is your gain!
You get more for your dollar.
Stretch your dollar.
Pick up a bargain.
You'll never find another bargain like this one!
It's clearly a better value.
How's that for value?
Get ready to pay a whole lot less for _____.
Get ready for fantastic savings.
Save on _____ costs.
Lower your _____ bills.

energy-smart
like getting three _____s for the price of one
everything you'd expect from a high-priced _____
    —for a lot less
Buy only the ones you want.
Order just the ones you need.
You pay only when . . .
no wasted expense
cost-efficient
cost-effective
a full-time staff at part-time cost
cuts your costs dramatically
helps you avoid costly mistakes
eliminates costly _____
cuts your overhead costs
trims your _____ costs
. . . on a shoestring budget
if you're on a tight budget . . .
within budget
money-saving ideas
money-saving opportunity
a modest investment

For further inspiration, see:
Sale/Discount (Part 1)
All-Purpose Grabbers (Part 1)

NEW / ADVANCED

Introducing . . .
Coming soon:
just published
just released
just arrived
now available
fresh
sleek new
shiny new
factory-sealed
fresh off the press
newly issued
newly minted
mint condition
brand new
brand spanking new
amazing new
bold new
remarkable new
the new look in _____
the latest look in _____
the latest _____
innovative
contemporary
modern
ultramodern
futuristic
startling
unprecedented

revolutionary
breakthrough
groundbreaking
trailblazing
state-of-the-art
cutting-edge
high-performance
high-tech
precision-engineered
technologically advanced
scientifically designed
21st century
up-to-date
up-to-the-minute
current
topical
updated
sophisticated
newly discovered
exciting _____ discovery
new miracle _____
the latest _____ technology
today's _____
designed for today's _____
keeps pace with . . .
stays on top of . . .
in the vanguard of . . .
makes the _____ obsolete
the next generation of _____

the latest breakthrough in _____

the most exciting _____ breakthrough in
  over _____ years

something new and exciting

an exciting new way to . . .

the first and only _____

the first _____ to . . .

the world's first _____

a revolution in _____

a breakthrough in _____

the successor to _____

a radical departure

a novel approach

a wave of innovation

technological wizardry

creative vision

pioneering spirit

into new territory

ahead of its time

We've redefined . . .

We rewrote the rules...

addressing tomorrow's business needs today

tomorrow's _____

the _____ of tomorrow

the _____ of the future

You'll know you've seen the future.

where everything is happening

available for the first time

another first

a fresh new approach to _____

a whole new world of _____

the new look in _____

a totally new concept in _____

something new and different

a fresh new twist

a fresh new face

a great new idea

a new era in _____

a new way of looking at _____

takes _____ to a whole new level

Don't _____ today with yesterday's _____.

For further inspiration, see:

Improved

Timely

PLAIN / NATURAL

raw
pure
unrefined
simple
fresh
wholesome
good
honest
true
solid
real
genuine
decent
modest
humble
innocent
sincere
plainspoken
straightforward
earthy
hearty
rough-hewn
homespun
homemade
homegrown
home-baked
down-home

down-to-earth
small-town
folksy
friendly
neighborly
soulful
congenial
comforting
unpretentious
unaffected
unassuming
unostentatious
unfussy
uncluttered
unadorned
unembellished
unvarnished
unadulterated
untainted
unsullied
unspoiled
unchanged
untamed
untouched by . . .
pristine
virgin
primeval

wild
free
healthful
bracing
refreshing
refreshingly _____
all-natural
as nature intended
Get back to nature . . .
You can still see/taste/smell/hear/
    feel/experience the . . .
not fancier, just better
just the facts
nothing added
no harsh chemicals
fragrance-free
_____-free

For further inspiration, see:
Authentic
Comfortable
Fresh/Wholesome
Honest
Reliable
Traditional/Classic

PLEASURE/SATISFACTION

enjoyment
joy
pure joy
bliss
sheer bliss
delight
ecstasy
heaven
paradise
enchantment
happiness
contentment
fulfillment
harmony
inner peace
deeply satisfying
emotionally engaging
soothing
pleasing
gratifying
fulfilling
stirring
alluring
captivating
delightful

entertaining
revives you
energizes you
will delight you
will dazzle you
You'll be tickled . . .
You'll be enthralled . . .
You'll be enchanted . . .
You'll love . . .
You'll enjoy . . .
You'll appreciate . . .
Your spirit will go "ahhh" . . .
Try a little self-indulgence for a
    change.
Imagine the fun you'll have . . .
the time of your life
your passport to . . .
your ticket to . . .
entertains while it . . .
enjoyment for years to come . . .
years of fun and pleasure
countless hours of entertainment
fun for the whole family
Get more out of . . .
satisfies your hunger

Taste the difference!
revives your senses
makes you feel good all over
makes you feel brand-new again
blissed-out
. . . to your heart's content
made for you to enjoy
Sit back and enjoy . . .
Reward yourself with a _____.
delightful to give or receive
everything you've always
    wanted in a _____
You couldn't ask for a
    better _____.
You'll love the way it . . .
satisfies your need for . . .
We're not satisfied until you are.

For further inspiration, see:
Appealing
Comfortable
Exciting/Stimulating
Fun/Cheerful
Sensory Qualities
Guarantees (Part 3)

POPULAR

acclaimed
best-selling
favorite
perennial favorite
all-time favorite
America's favorite _____
_____'s favorite _____
_____'s most requested _____
_____'s best-loved _____
famous
famed
renowned
acclaimed
hailed
praised
honored
admired
beloved
illustrious
legendary
celebrated
triumphant
successful
thriving
up-and-coming
on the rise
out of control
booming

record-breaking
in vogue
sizzling
smokin'
the hottest
influential
highly regarded
held in high regard
the _____ sensation
the _____ phenomenon
the _____ Age
word-of-mouth
buzz
enjoys a huge following
preferred over all other _____s
preferred by more . . .
attended by more . . .
bought by more . . .
recommended by more . . .
approved by . . .
endorsed by . . .
chosen by . . .
eagerly awaited
always in demand
must-have
widespread acceptance
one of the most talked-about
     _____s

Everybody's talking about _____.
Everybody's discovering _____
More and more _____ are
     discovering _____.
Everybody loves _____.
Everybody wants to see _____.
a winner
a superstar
star power
a blockbuster
a box-office smash
smash hit
has taken _____ by storm
Now in its _____ week!
the hottest _____ in town
a hot property
buzzworthy
the people's choice
more popular than ever
as big as Elvis
a phenomenal success
a success story
You can't argue with success.

For further inspiration, see:
Appealing
Distinguished/Status
Stylish

POWERFUL

dramatic
spectacular
explosive
dynamite
a knockout
gut-wrenching
bone-crushing
high-powered
industrial-strength
maximum-strength
revved-up
souped-up
turbocharged
hard-driving
hard-hitting
high-energy
intense
assertive
aggressive
in-your-face
potent
mighty
raging
rampaging
dynamic
vibrant
forceful
searing
elemental

high-voltage
electric
electrifying
overpowering
overwhelming
earthshaking
titanic
heavyweight
muscular
brawny
beefy
rugged
robust
tough
tough-as-nails
masterful
commanding
compelling
staggering
relentless
riveting
hypnotic
mesmerizing
shocking
stunning
stuns
shocks
ignites
bursts

erupts
explodes
blasts
shatters
smashes
slams
slaps
blows away . . .
packs a wallop
packs a punch
blows the lid off
never lets up
sweeps you along
knocks your socks off
a knockout punch
a powder keg
heavy artillery
full throttle
jet-propelled
horsepower
fuel-injected
running on all cylinders
high-performance
vitality
vigor
energy
juice
mojo
juju

impact
primitive power
raw power
twice the power of _____
powered by . . .
fueled by . . .
propelled by . . .
built like a tank
like a sumo wrestler
like a charging rhino

like a bull elephant
a tidal wave
a tsunami
a cyclone
a whirlwind
a blizzard
an Arctic blast
hurricane force
Unleash the power of . . .
Amp it up . . .

Rock your _____.
Stoke your inner fires.
Turbocharge your _____.

For further inspiration, see:
Durable/Solid
Exciting/Stimulating
Results/Performance

RELIABLE

proven/time-proven
tested/time-tested
authoritative
dependable
honest
faithful
trusted
trustworthy
unerring
unswerving
steady
steadfast
stalwart
stable
practical
functional
surefire
no-nonsense
established
approved
safe
sound
secure
childproof
_____proof
guaranteed to . . .
stands up to . . .
comes to grips with . . .
our proven method of . . .

proven strategies/techniques
gets the job done when you need it
long-lasting
will serve you faithfully
will last for generations
lasts a lifetime
a lifetime companion
a lifetime of satisfaction
actually improves with age
carefully tested
clinically tested
laboratory tested
individually tested
scientifically formulated
precision engineered
made to our exacting specifications
quality controlled
goes through rigorous testing
rigorous standards
stringent standards
We don't cut corners.
the quality you've come to expect
our commitment to quality
no compromising on quality
no shortcuts
solid workmanship
smooth performance
unfailing accuracy
error-free

trouble-free
maintenance-free
won't quit
_____ can handle it
a proven track record
for over _____ years
never lets you down
top credentials
a name you can trust
the most trusted name in _____
has stood the test of time
We've won a loyal following . . .
recommended/endorsed/
    approved by . . .
You can count/rely/depend
    on _____.
_____ you can count/rely/
    depend on.
Over _____ million satisfied
    customers depend on _____.
Depend on it!

For further inspiration, see:
Authentic
Durable/Solid
Experienced/Expert
Honest
Results/Performance
Security/Peace of Mind

RESULTS/PERFORMANCE

effective

efficient

productive

powerful

successful

tested

proven

high-performing

hardworking

fast-acting

acts

accomplishes

performs

outperforms

solves

produces

makes

establishes

delivers

improves

increases

boosts

raises

lowers

reduces

cuts down on

fights

combats

tackles

zaps

foils

beats

kills

wipes out

stamps out

stops

halts

maintains

provides

furnishes

restores

replenishes

rejuvenates

revitalizes

protects

prevents

creates

corrects

fixes

pays off

does the job

does what it's designed to do

never lets you down

never lets up

won't loaf on the job

won't quit

comes through in the crunch

gets results

works immediately

works wonders

works like magic

makes the difference

gets rid of annoying _____

puts an end to _____

cuts through _____

whisks away _____

sniffs out _____

prolongs the life of _____

brings out the beauty
      of _____

ends unsightly _____

tackles the dirtiest jobs

does it all

winning performance

unmatched performance

for even sweeter performance

high-performance _____

instant ____

immediate results

fast results

remarkable results

proven results

It really works!

gets the job done

success guaranteed

guaranteed safe and effective

You can count on _____.

Compare for yourself.
Find out for yourself.
Watch it go to work!
Say good-bye to _____.
Say good riddance
   to _____.
Get rid of _____ for good.
The proof is in the . . .
outperforms the competition

does more with less
changes unproductive habits
boosts morale
builds motivation
increases productivity
helps you build a top-performing
   team
turns ordinary _____ into
   powerful _____

Mission accomplished!

For further inspiration, see:
Competitive
Durable/Solid
Experienced/Expert
Reliable
Service/Help

ROMANTIC

passionate
breathless
intimate
kindled
burning
smoldering
torrid
tempestuous
rapturous
ravishing
dashing
giddy
dizzy
smitten
blissful
head-over-heels
spirited
bold
reckless
love
romance
lifelong romance
infatuation
crush
sheer bliss
dreams

fantasies
fireworks
rendezvous
secret tryst
love affair
candlelight
a bouquet of roses
the scent of perfume
purple dusk
a deserted beach
a secluded retreat
a crackling fireplace
soft music
rain on the roof
a torrid tango
a sultry samba
exchanged glances
holding hands
whispered intimacies
first kiss
a tender caress
sultry nights
one special person
enchanting
haunting
enthralling

evocative
captivating
mystical
magical
mysterious
dreamlike
a grand gesture
a wondrous journey
enchanted places
Set the mood for . . .
Enter a timeless realm of . . .
Surrender to the spell of . . .
Fall in love all over again.
creates an aura of . . .
the mystique of . . .
the eternal mystery of . . .
life's most treasured moments
the romance of . . .
a token of your affection
_____ for lovers

For further inspiration, see:
Appealing
Sensory Qualities
Sexy
Traditional/Classic

SECURITY/ PEACE OF MIND

safe
secure
snug
relaxing
soothing
secluded
protected
full protection
strictly confidential
total security
total privacy
a haven of . . .
a refuge
a sanctuary
a safe place
shelters you from . . .
insulates you . . .
protects you . . .
protects your valuable _____
protects your investment
fully protects . . .
shields you from . . .
guards against . . .
locks out . . .
defends your . . .
alerts you . . .
ever-vigilant
a constant reminder
your assurance of . . .

your guarantee of . . .
your defense against . . .
stops _____ in their tracks
totally safe
guaranteed safe and effective
safe and painless
built-in safety features
nonskid surface
nonslip grip
childproof
_____proof
allergy-tested
safety-tested
shuts off automatically
takes care of itself
carefree
worry-free
trouble-free
maintenance-free
no headaches
Never again will you have to . . .
Avoid embarrassing mistakes . . .
prevents costly and embarrassing
    errors
gives you the assurance of . . .
puts your mind at ease
saves you needless worry
You won't lose any more sleep
    over _____.

You'll never have to take chances
    with _____.
Why take chances with _____?
Relax!
Take it easy!
Sleep secure.
Rest easy.
You'll rest easier.
Ease your mind.
You can depend/count/rely
    on . . .
no more guesswork
a lifetime of _____
lets you forget about . . .
. . . so you feel more secure
    than ever.
You're in control.
_____ with confidence.
We're always there when you
    need us.
Your _____ can never be
    canceled.
lifetime warranty

For further inspiration, see:
Choice/Control
Reliable
Results/Performance
Guarantees (Part 3)

SELF-IMPROVEMENT

self-expression
self-esteem
self-confidence
self-empowerment
self-mastery
life-enriching
life-enhancing
personal growth
wisdom
harmony
fulfillment
rewards
knowledge
education
a golden opportunity
a once-in-a-lifetime opportunity
new opportunities for . . .
virtually limitless opportunities
your chance to . . .
opens the way to . . .
Recapture your . . .
Unlock your . . .
Unblock your . . .
Release your . . .
Tap into your . . .
Take control of your . . .
Pursue your . . .
Follow your . . .
Build your . . .

Improve your . . .
Boost your . . .
Discover the . . .
Achieve . . .
Win . . .
Create . . .
Move ahead . . .
You owe yourself . . .
You can do it!
Go for it!
your best self
a new you
feel brand-new
awakens your spirit
empowers you to . . .
enhances your . . .
unleashes your creativity
taps your inner strength
programs your subconscious
gives you a whole new perspective
helps you avoid the pitfalls
arms you with vital insights
builds your self-confidence
Gain hands-on experience . . .
Pick up vital new skills . . .
Fine-tune your _____ skills.
skills you'll use your whole life long
powerful strategies for taking charge of . . .
your blueprint for achievement

_____ can be the key to your success.
We'll stretch your mind.
You learn by doing.
practical, hands-on training
gives you a clear advantage
gives you the competitive edge
keeps you ahead of the game
helps you work smarter, not harder
helps you achieve more in less time
gets you in on the ground floor
helps you and your organization . . .
You start with _____ and quickly move
    on to _____.
Discover your hidden talents.
a chance to use your talents
Unlock your potential.
Remove mental blocks to success.
the road to success
secrets of success
Visualize your success.
Be the success you were meant to be.
Wake up the _____ inside you.
Turn stress to your advantage.
Turn fear into confidence.
Achieve virtually any goal you envision.
Create healthy, winning habits.
Create more time in your schedule for the things
    that matter.

Turn your free time into learning time.
Take a lesson from the superstars.
Take the first step toward a happier, more
    productive life.
a happier and more fulfilling life
a more satisfying life
In _____ weeks you can be on your
    way to . . .
Turn your life around.
You'll feel great about yourself.
You'll feel as good as you look.
You'll look as good as you feel.
Win admiring glances . . .
Imagine the possibilities . . .
Invest in yourself.
an investment in your future
will change your life
Live your dreams _now_.
You've dreamed about it. Now you can
    do it!
You'll be glad you did.

For further inspiration, see:
Exciting/Stimulating
Healthful
Informative
Money-Making
Heads and Slogans (Part 1)

SENSORY QUALITIES

hue
shade
muted colors
understated colors
pastel shades
soft colors
vivid hues
rich palette
vibrant colors
warm colors
hot colors
cool colors
sensuous colors
tropical colors
sun-drenched colors
desert colors
colors of the sea
earth tones
skin tones
a medley of color
a rainbow of color
an explosion of color
a burst of color
multicolored
iridescent
transparent
translucent
sheer

see-through
shapely
contoured
streamlined
sleek
satiny
silky
velvety
slinky
lithe
lean
slender
slim
ripe
warm
balmy
radiant
sunny
fiery
scorching
smoldering
hot
white-hot
heat
steaming
windswept
crystalline
icy

chilled
brisk
cool
textured
crinkly
crisp
serrated
weathered
craggy
woolly
stubbly
pebbly
gritty
sandy
fine-grained
smooth
oily
creamy
buttery
sharp
metallic
flaky
flecked
burnished
a rich patina
lustrous
gleaming
luminous

incandescent
glowing
shimmering
moonlit
sunlit
earthy
billowing
soft
fleecy
feathery
downy
wispy
gossamer
misty
a fine mist
moist
liquid
wet
spray
frothy
bubbling
foamy
effervescent
sparkling
glittering
glimmering
glistening
gemlike
brilliant
bright
firm
full-bodied
solid
many-sided

oblong
square
cubic
cylindrical
cone-shaped
heart-shaped
rounded
oval
circular
spherical
globe-shaped
harmonious
clean
muted
fragrant
scented
bouquet
flowery
mossy
musky
smoky
incense
the scent of roses/lilacs/
   lavender/honeysuckle/
   pine/cedar/lemons/
   oranges/salty sea air
savory
mouthwatering
tasty
salty
tangy
tart
sour
sharp

bitter
sweet
bittersweet
pungent
crisp
crunchy
chewy
tender
juicy
zesty
seasoned
luscious
delicious
succulent
ambrosial
melodious
resonant
echoing
ringing
jingling
chiming
trilling
warbling
whistling
thundering
rumbling
crackling
sizzling
fizzing
gurgling
hissing
humming
droning
whirring

purring	slap	*For further inspiration, see:*
whispering	bang	**Appealing**
quiet	zoom	**Fresh/Wholesome**
silent	boom	**Good-Looking**
crash	blast	**Pleasure/Satisfaction**
smash	pop	**Sexy**
smack	snap	
whack	zap	
thud	whoosh	

Note: Look for more comprehensive lists of sensory images (Color, Fragrance, Sound, Taste, Texture) in *More Words That Sell.*

SERVICE / HELP

helpful
helps you . . .
lets you . . .
enables you to . . .
permits you to . . .
assists you . . .
reviews
evaluates
simplifies
clarifies
facilitates
monitors
advises
consults
partners
creates
develops
protects
solves
fixes
accomplishes
performs
implements
delivers
We deliver . . .
Free delivery!
We ship worldwide . . .
same-day shipping
next-day delivery

delivered to your door
right to your doorstep
the answer to all your _____ needs
addresses your needs
Our job is to help you . . .
That's what we give you.
That's where we come in.
We do the work for you.
our proven method of . . .
our proven expertise
proven techniques for . . .
time-saving techniques
the solution to your . . .
sound advice on how to . . .
valuable tips
instant feedback
prompt service
free same-day installation
professional advice
personal advice
guides you every step of the way
takes the guesswork out of _____
helps you avoid the pitfalls
You can turn to us with confidence.
We come through for you . . .
We come through in the crunch.
a real lifesaver
We make it easier for you to . . .
Let _____ show you the right way to . . .

Let _____ plan and manage your _____.
We'll pamper you.
We handle the job from start to finish.
We're in business to help your business succeed.
Our real business is *you*.
We're always at your service.
a good friend to have by your side
your partner in _____
_____ won't let you down.
You can count on _____.
_____ gets the job done when you need it.
what you need, when you need it
whenever and wherever
around the clock
24/7
24/7/365
We make an effort to . . .
We do it all for you.
We cater to...
We come to grips with . . .
Your _____ gets top-priority treatment.
We provide training and support.
We provide the highest level of customer service.

Our associates are trained to help you . . .
Our friendly staff is ready to assist you.
. . . to serve you better
Each of our dealers is hand-picked . . .
Your _____ dealer works with you . . .
Your _____ dealer takes the time and effort to . . .
At _____, we do all that and more.
We'll meet all your requirements.
We offer a full range of . . .
breadth of service
one-stop assistance
firsthand briefing
our professional opinion
powerful solutions
our commitment to our clients/customers
a total management package

For further inspiration, see:
Convenient
Experienced/Expert
Reliable
Results/Performance

SEXY

sassy
flirty
tempting
tantalizing
seductive
alluring
provocative
daring
shocking
reckless
naughty
forbidden
wicked
shameless
sinful
scandalous
hot
sultry
steamy
smoldering
sizzling
scorching
torrid
passionate
intimate
delicate
sensuous
slinky
slender

lean
lithe
sleek
supple
shapely
ripe
voluptuous
luscious
tender
moist
creamy
musky
earthy
flowing
silky
satiny
velvety
sheer
diaphanous
see-through
bare
undressed
naked
nude
flesh
skin
lips
kiss
seduce

caress
touch
fondle
curves
contours
swaying
dancing
aching
churning
throbbing
craving
desire
lust
fire
flame
passion
pleasure
delight
frolic
ecstasy
fireworks
feminine
ultrafeminine
temptress
seductress
enchantress
goddess
babe
hottie

coquette
nymph
pixie
masculine
macho
brawny
muscular
firm
sinewy
fleshy
shamelessly _____

sinfully _____
decadently _____
like a long, slow kiss
like a slow dance in the dark
the sway of her hips
sun and sand
slightly sinful
decidedly sinful
forbidden pleasures
naked passion
sultry nights

loaded with sex appeal
Feel the energy . . .
Feel the rhythms . . .

For further inspiration, see:
Appealing
Exciting/Stimulating
Good-Looking
Pleasure/Satisfaction
Romantic
Sensory Qualities

SMALL / LESS

little

miniature

miniaturized

mini_____

micro_____

nano_____

minimal/minimalist

minuscule

tiny

petite

cute little . . .

elfin

midget

dwarf

Lilliputian

diminutive

compact

conveniently compact

compact styling

neat

concise

succinct

brief

cozy

intimate

on an intimate scale

vest-pocket

pocket-sized

_____ in your pocket

purse-sized

fits easily in your _____

slips easily into your _____

fits anywhere

won't crowd your _____

takes up only _____ of space

its small footprint saves space

space-saving

portable

handheld

fits in the palm of your hand

Take it wherever you go.

go-anywhere

economy of scale

lean

thin/ultrathin

slim/ultraslim

trim

a dash of . . .

a pinch of . . .

a little bit of . . .

just a dollop of . . .

a *soupçon* of . . .

small and light

lightweight

featherweight

light as a feather

weighs a scant _____ ounces

no bulky _____

won't weigh you down

lightens your load

unobtrusive

discreet

undetectable

hides easily

fits comfortably in . . .

easily concealed

stores easily in the smallest spaces

uses a minimum of space to
    deliver maximum benefits

a little giant

small wonder

compressed

reduced

pared

slashed

cut down

cut back

condensed

abridged

abbreviated

downsized

pared down

scaled down

trimmed down

reduced to a minimum

barely more than . . .

virtually nonexistent

SOPHISTICATED / SMART

polished
refined
elegant
stylish
chic
urbane
cosmopolitan
worldly
civilized
VIP
elite
educated
erudite
intelligent
bright
brilliant
ingenious
gifted
talented
intellectual
literate
articulate
eloquent
perceptive
discerning
wise
sensible
shrewd
clever

witty
droll
ironic
acerbic
keen
incisive
sharp
chic
uptown
well-bred
suave
impeccable
smooth
sleek
dapper
natty
debonair
jaded
hip
cool
drop-dead cool
simple elegance
classic elegance
finesse
savoir faire
savvy
smarts
expertise
professionalism

proficiency
intelligence
brainpower
ingenuity
advanced
intricate
complex
cutting-edge
the latest word in . . .
precision-engineered
high-performance
high-tech
technologically advanced
scientifically designed
cleverly designed
smart design
smart details
stunning complexity
next-generation
masters of . . .
inner circle
understated grace and elegance
for the discriminating few
for the most discerning critic
the thinking person's _____

For further inspiration, see:
Distinguished/Status
Stylish

STYLISH

fashionable

glamorous

chic

très chic

très belle

très cool

très hot

smart

elegant

well tailored

impeccably tailored

designer _____

coordinated

the right stuff

correct

tasteful

classic

retro

simple

elegantly simple

simply elegant

soft-spoken

subtle

low-key

tastefully understated

graceful

sporty

splashy

flashy

knockout

head-turning

attention-getting

drop-dead gorgeous

dressed to kill

to die for

wicked

hot

the hottest _____ in town

sizzling

smashing

ravishing

snappy

snazzy

spiffy

sassy

breezy

vibrant

dazzling

good-looking

new look

. . . with panache

. . . with flair

. . . with pizzazz

the last word in . . .

the latest

modish

current

trendy

trendsetting

now

in vogue

killer

electric

edgy

sleek

slinky

slim

slender

svelte

flattering

jaunty

dashing

dapper

debonair

suave

sophisticated

swank

natty

rakish

street-smart

audacious

flamboyant

outrageous

daring

bold

bold new look

fashion flair

a dash of panache
tailored to perfection
the epitome of elegance
classically proportioned
with style and grace
a study in _____
just the right touch of _____
the season's most wearable trend

goes with anything
Make your statement . . .
Transform your look with . . .
Dress up your look with . . .
Spiff yourself up . . .
Get ready to shine . . .
We've got your style.
It's now. It's *wow.*

For further inspiration, see:
Good-Looking
Luxurious
New/Advanced
Sexy
Sophisticated/Smart

SUITABLE

appropriate
proper
optimum
right
just right
just the thing for . . .
ideal for . . .
the best choice
perfect for . . .
a perfect match
the perfect fit for your needs
the perfect complement to . . .
the perfect reflection of your . . .
the perfect companion to . . .
the perfect _____
the ideal companion
fully compatible with . . .
works seamlessly with . . .
befitting your . . .
the ultimate in versatility
equally suitable for _____ or _____
infinitely adaptable
one size fits all
fits all standard _____

ideally sized
uniquely suited . . .
suits your lifestyle
for all your _____ needs
designed to suit your needs
geared to your needs
tailored to your needs
custom-tailored
custom-designed
customized to meet your needs
created especially for you
It was made for you.
uniquely yours
the _____ you were meant
   to _____
We're sure to have the perfect
   _____ for you.
You've come to the right place.
Try our _____ on for size.
the _____ you've been
   looking for
an expression of your . . .
It's the real you.
becomes you

fits you like a glove
custom-fitted
mirrors your . . .
meets your exacting standards
designed for the _____ in you
designed specifically for . . .
utilizes your existing _____
can be integrated with your
   existing _____
blends beautifully with
   your _____
a welcome addition to your
   collection
perfect for school, home,
   or office
perfect for _____ buffs
will delight _____ aficionados

For further inspiration, see:
Convenient
Gift
Timely
Useful/Practical

SUPERIOR

better/best
outstanding
exceptional
excellent
extraordinary
superb/super
supreme
distinguished
first-class/first-rate
highest quality
five-star quality
award-winning
brilliant
impeccable
perfect/picture-perfect
flawless
the finest . . .
the greatest . . .
the ultimate . . .
the foremost . . .
the leading . . .
the premier . . .
the top . . .
top-of-the-line
top-notch
tops
top-ranking
highest-ranking
matchless

unmatched
unrivaled
unequaled
unexcelled
unsurpassed
unparalleled
unbeatable
peerless
incomparable
outclasses
surpasses
excels
outranks
outshines
America's number one _____
America's leading _____
_____'s most acclaimed _____
the definitive _____
the ultimate _____
the epitome of _____
the summit
second to none
premium quality
simply the finest _____ you
   can buy
the crown jewel
recognized by experts
sets the industry standard
the best in the business

still the best
the undisputed leader
. . . of the highest stature
your number one source
sets the standard
in a class by itself
the standard by which
   other _____s are judged
a _____ of distinction
serious _____
Nobody beats . . .
Nobody else comes close.
_____ rules!
kicks butt
No other _____ offers . . .
the better way to . . .
more than all others combined
transcends the common _____
often imitated but never equaled
second to none
as good as it gets
There's simply no comparison.
Don't settle for anything less.
There's no substitute for _____.

For further inspiration, see:
Distinguished/Status
Luxurious
Part 4 (Pages 103–110)

TIMELY

prompt
punctual
quick
speedy
immediate
on time
on time, all the time
always on time
quick turnaround
fast results
instant _____
in seconds
in minutes
in days
in a matter of weeks
updated regularly
updated every hour/day/week/month
always stays current
up-to-the-minute
stays on top of . . .
keeps pace with . . .
keeps abreast of . . .
never out of date
for any occasion
whenever you want it
whenever and wherever you need it
gives you what you want, when you want it
what you need, when you need it

just when you need it most
long-needed
long-awaited
long overdue
a welcome addition to . . .
It's finally here.
Finally, a . . .
At last there's a . . .
the _____ whose time has come
Now's the time for . . .
There's never been a better time for . . .
It was only a matter of time.
Just when you thought . . .
just in time for _____
It's about time . . .
Isn't it time . . . ?
There's no time like now.
came along at just the right time
the first _____ to address the problems of . . .
Our timing couldn't have been better.
Our timing is right on the mark.

For further inspiration, see:
Convenient

Fast

Improved

New/Advanced

Suitable

TRADITIONAL / CLASSIC

historic
vintage
timeless
time-honored
age-old
centuries-old
antique
venerable
treasured
civilized
lasting
enduring
immortal
storied
legendary
evocative
nostalgic
long-forgotten
never-to-be-forgotten
quaint
old-fashioned
picturesque
gracious
charming
sentimental
souvenir
legacy
heritage
keepsake

a treasured heirloom
tomorrow's heirlooms
heirloom-quality
a cherished reminder
in the rich tradition of . . .
old-world craftsmanship
faithfully crafted
hallmarks of . . .
the storied past
a nostalgic glimpse of . . .
evokes a world of . . .
the beauty of a vanished world
the grace and charm of a
    bygone era
makes the past come alive
History comes alive.
lets you relive . . .
the beauty of _____ lives on
a reminder of your heritage
We've stayed true to our
    heritage . . .
masterpieces
old masters
the lasting legacy of . . .
the roots of . . .
in the beginning . . .
It's an old _____ custom.
richly restored
faithfully reproduced

faithfully recreates . . .
authentic in every detail
timeless style
never goes out of style
classically simple
classically elegant
understated elegance
elegant retro look
enduring beauty
enduring quality
living classics
They still speak to us today.
Rediscover . . .
Savor the memories . . .
You *can* go home again.
Come home to _____.
Remember how you loved _____?
_____ from your past
the same _____ you grew up with
the same _____ your
    grandparents loved
We've found them again for you.
just the way you remember it
the same way we've been making
    it for _____ years

For further inspiration, see:
Authentic
Made

UNUSUAL

original
unique
special
distinctive
different
remarkable
exceptional
extraordinary
rare
scarce
uncommon
unprecedented
unparalleled
incomparable
matchless
fantastic
imaginative
daring
unconventional
slightly eccentric
wild and crazy
maverick
renegade
practically illegal
offbeat
exotic
strange
mysterious
mystifying

magical
the only . . .
the one and only . . .
the first and only . . .
the only one of its kind
one of a kind . . .
unlike any other . . .
No two are alike.
as individual as you are
as individual as your fingerprints
personalized just for you
utterly original
our patented _____
our exclusive _____
our signature _____
in a class by itself
out of the ordinary
a different kind of _____
delightfully different
dramatically different
dares to be different
_____ with a difference
. . . with a different spirit
something new and different
a fresh approach to . . .
a refreshing change of pace
_____ with a twist!
a conversation starter
There's nothing quite like it.

There's no other _____ like _____.
There's never been anything
    like _____.
No other _____ comes close.
limited edition
limited to _____ copies
uniquely suited to . . .
specially formulated
custom-designed
custom-tailored
custom-made
customized
hard to find
a rare find
off the beaten track
We searched far and wide for
    these . . .
one of those _____ you
    encounter only a few times
    during your life
You've never seen a _____
    like this.
Nobody else gives you . . .
A _____ exclusive!
Only _____ brings you . . .
available only from _____
not available anywhere else at
    any price
not available in any store

USEFUL / PRACTICAL

functional
helpful
handy
convenient
sensible
basic
simple
unfussy
streamlined
applicable
adaptable
flexible
versatile
universal
multipurpose
ingenious
clever
worthwhile
ideal for _____
perfect for _____
everyday _____
serves as a _____
serves a useful purpose
more than a _____
doubles as a _____
can serve as a _____ as well as a _____
performs double duty as a _____ and a _____
converts into a _____
the ultimate in versatility

dozens of uses
hundreds of uses
infinitely useful
infinitely adaptable
all-purpose
for every purpose
The possibilities are endless.
a rugged performer
down-to-earth
unpretentious
no-nonsense
no-frills
just the basics
just the essentials
no more or less than you need
full of functional features
as functional as it is handsome
functional beauty
fast and easy to use
Use it over and over again.
You'll never run out of uses for this _____.
Why spend top dollar on _____ when all
   you need is _____?

For further inspiration, see:
Convenient
Plain/Natural
Suitable
Valuable

VALUABLE

invaluable
important
indispensable
worthwhile
worthy
a must
a necessity
a lifesaver
essential
basic
integral
critical
vital
fundamental
prized
treasured
cherished
revered
exquisite
choice
rare
scarce
precious

expensive
costly
rare and costly
priceless
matchless
incomparable
a masterpiece
irreplaceable
inestimable value
incalculable value
deluxe
luxe
luxurious
high-priced
high-ticket
upmarket
upscale
museum quality
limited edition
the foundation of . . .
an integral part of . . .
a vital link
a precious commodity

no expense has been spared
rare beauty
the epitome of . . .
a _____ of distinction
a _____ you'll be proud
   to own
the finest _____ of its kind
rewarding
beneficial
profitable
pays off
a wise investment
a smart investment
an investment in your future
a valued addition to your . . .
a valued member of . . .
You'll wonder how you ever got
   along without it.

For further inspiration, see:
Indispensable
Luxurious
Superior

PART 3

CLINCHERS
CLOSING STATEMENTS THAT MOTIVATE YOUR AUDIENCE TO RESPOND

PERSUADING
YOUR AUDIENCE

Without a doubt, . . .

In short, this _____ will help you . . .

You get all these benefits:

Start reaping the benefits today.

It's a small investment that will deliver
tremendous benefits.

It just might be the best investment you'll
ever make.

It just might make your life richer than
ever before.

Try a _____ for one year and see how much
it gives you in return.

Why settle for _____ when you can have _____?

You can't lose.

What have you got to lose?

In short, you have nothing to lose.

This is the opportunity you've been waiting for.

Let this be the year you finally . . .

Don't go on wondering if you could have . . .

A rewarding _____ awaits you.

Can you think of any reason *not* to send for
your _____?

Ask yourself if you can afford not to . . .

You owe it to your family to . . .

Frankly, I can't understand why everybody
doesn't take advantage of this offer.

I think you'll find that . . .

I think you'll agree . . .

We stand behind our claims.

We're ready to prove everything we claim.

Of course, your gift is tax-deductible.

I know you receive appeals from many good
causes, but I can't think of a better cause
than _____.

Please join us in the fight for/against _____.
Together we can . . .

But we can't do it without you.

Does all this sound too good to be true?

You'll still be able to do it your way—
only better!

Before you buy a _____, find out what _____
has to offer.

You'll wonder how you ever managed without it.

We're sure to have the perfect _____ for you.

You won't be disappointed.

Put our _____ to the test.

But the real payoff comes when . . .

That's all it takes to . . .

All this can be yours.

Take as many as you wish—or none at all!

You can see for yourself that . . .

Once you try us, you'll want to stay with us.

Discover why our customers keep coming
back for more.

Quantities are limited, so act now.

Our supply is limited.

We expect the _____ to be selling out quickly
at this low price.

Take your pick now, while these amazing
   prices are still in effect.
This special offer is available for a limited
   time only.
Only by taking advantage of this offer now
   can you receive . . .
This invitation cannot be extended again.
Please don't miss out!
Don't miss this unusual opportunity.
But we can only hold your reservation for
   _____ days.
In the end, all that matters is . . .
Remember, time is running out.
Remember, _____ is available exclusively
   from us.
You won't find it in any store.
Take advantage of this special offer while it lasts.

You'll be glad you did.
Try to imagine the alternative.
Think of what you have to look forward to.
You've waited long enough.
You'll wonder why you waited.
The sooner you act, the sooner your _____ begins.
. . . and that's a promise!
There's just one conclusion:
_____ is the obvious choice.
It's no wonder that we're the number
   one choice . . .

For further inspiration, see:
Minimizing Risk
The Moment of Decision
Guarantees

MINIMIZING RISK

Our offer is simple:

Send no money!

Send no money now.

Send no payment now.

No risk now, no risk later!

It's yours for a full month risk-free.

No risk! No obligation!

You're under no obligation.

No obligation to buy anything ever!

A simple invitation with no strings attached.

You may cancel at any time.

Say "yes" now and decide later.

Test our _____ for _____ days—*then* decide.

Use it for _____ days at our expense.

Try _____ at our risk.

Try us for _____ months.

We'll send you _____ to examine FREE—with no cost, obligation, or commitment.

We won't bill you for _____ days.

If you decide to keep it, pay just $_____.

Choose only the _____ you want.

Keep only the _____ you want.

Feel free to cancel at any time.

There's absolutely no risk on your part. Just the promise of . . .

There's absolutely no obligation on your part.

There's no cost or commitment on your part.

You don't risk a cent.

You never risk a cent.

Ordering from _____ is totally risk-free.

You risk nothing.

Send us your no-risk RSVP today.

If you decide it's not for you, pay nothing and keep the _____ with our compliments.

Simply return it to us and owe nothing.

It costs nothing . . . you owe nothing.

Remember, you pay nothing in advance.

The cost of your _____ is totally refundable.

No questions asked.

We'll buy it back from you.

No purchase necessary.

No salespeople will call.

You have so much to gain and absolutely nothing to lose.

What have you got to lose?

It won't cost you anything to find out.

Just give us a fair trial.

All I'm asking is that you give us a try.

Simply *try* . . .

You can always change your mind later.

For further inspiration, see:

Guarantees

Trial Offer/No Obligation (Part 1)

THE MOMENT
OF DECISION

Interested?
Intrigued?
Convinced?
This is your moment.
It's time for action.
Now is the best time.
Don't wait any longer.
Don't hesitate.
Don't miss out.
Don't miss this opportunity.
Don't miss the action!
Don't risk losing your _____.
Why wait another day?
You've waited long enough.
We're expecting you.
I invite you . . .
With your approval, I'd like to . . .
Now it's time for you to decide.
But enough from us. Now it's your turn.
Your move.
Take this important first step.
You decide.
See for yourself.
Say "yes" to . . .
Act now.
Take the plunge!
Get started now.
Please join us today.
But don't just take our word for it. Find out
for yourself.
But the only way to prove the value of _____
is to try it yourself.
You'll just have to experience it for yourself.
Try us.
Get to know us.
Put our ideas to work.
Rather than simply reading about it, why
don't you . . . ?
You be the judge.
It's time to make your choice.
You've got an important decision to make.
Make a resolution right now to . . .
It's up to you.
Time's running out.
Any delay will make it much harder to . . .
Don't delay!
Do it today!
But do it now!
See if we're not everything we promise to be.
You have absolutely nothing to lose.
So, if you're thinking, "Maybe I should," please do!
You simply can't lose.
Reserve your _____ today!
You'll be glad you did.

For further inspiration, see:
Persuading Your Audience
The Call to Action

THE CALL
TO ACTION

I invite you to . . .

Right now, I'm inviting you to . . .

I urge you to act at once.

I urge you to reply today.

It's important that you respond promptly.

I can't wait to hear from you.

We'd like to hear from you.

Please send us your contribution today.

Place your order by phone or e-mail. But do it today.

Apply online, call _____, or complete and mail the enclosed form today.

Just hit Reply and we'll e-mail you the details.

Sign up online at _____.com/_____.

Learn more about us at _____.com.

Click *here* to find out more about _____.

To avoid disappointment, be sure to place your order today.

Order now, while there's still time.

I must receive your order before the date shown.

To reserve your _____, . . .

It's not every day you get an invitation to _____, so order now.

Place your order now, while everything is still in front of you.

In a hurry? Call _____.

For even faster service, call _____.

To place your order, call us toll-free at _____.

Just reach for your phone.

_____ is just a phone call away.

Call our toll-free number today so you don't miss out on this remarkable offer.

We're waiting for your call.

Return the enclosed postage-paid card today, before it slips your mind.

Just complete and mail the enclosed postage-paid card—I'll do the rest.

To take advantage of this remarkable opportunity, simply fill out and return the enclosed card.

An order form is enclosed for your convenience.

Just fill out the convenient order form.

Please return it to me at your earliest convenience.

I urge you to send for our free catalog (brochure).

I urge you to look at the enclosed catalog (brochure).

Send for our colorful catalog.

Send for our free catalog.

Mail your order today!

Mail this convenient coupon today!

Send in your application today!

Call or e-mail us with your order today!

Write for our free illustrated brochure.

For more details call your . . .

Why not give us a call and find out more about us?

Please don't hesitate to call us.

Call us this week to schedule an appointment.

We look forward to hearing from you.

Ask your _____ dealer.

Call _____ to set up an appointment.

One of our friendly representatives will visit you at your convenience. Call _____ today.

Your _____ dealer has all the details. Call or e-mail us today!

Come in and introduce yourself. Call . . .

Come visit us at your convenience. Call . . .

Come in and let us show you around. Call . . .

Hurry in for a free demonstration. Call us at _____.

For a free demonstration, call _____.

Call _____ for your free evalulation.

I'll start your service as soon as I hear from you.

May I hear from you soon?

I can't wait to hear from you.

If you've already responded to this offer, pass it along to a friend.

For further inspiration, see:

The Moment of Decision

Order Information

THE P.S.

To claim your free _____, simply . . .

Want to save even more?

There's even more:

Remember, . . .

Don't forget:

While you're at it, . . .

Did you know that . . . ?

There's still time for you to . . .

I should also mention that . . .

Let me emphasize that . . .

If you need a more persuasive reason to give us the green light, please read the accompanying note from _____.

If you act now, you'll also receive . . .

Don't send any money now.

For fastest service, . . .

Apply online at _____.com and start reaping the benefits even sooner!

These _____s will be going fast. So please send us your order today!

Please use the enclosed reply form to send us your order today.

Thanks again. I look forward to hearing from you.

We'll mail your _____ as soon as we receive your order.

Once we receive your payment, we'll immediately reinstate your _____.

Remember, you must respond by _____ to qualify for this special offer.

Even if you don't plan to join now, . . .

If you have a friend or relative who might benefit from this offer, . . .

If you're already using a _____, why not pass this offer along to a friend or colleague?

For further inspiration, see:
The Call to Action

THE LIFT NOTE

If you've decided not to order, please read this
brief note.

Not ready to order? Please read this note.

Please do not open unless you have already
decided NOT to order.

Frankly, I'm puzzled.

I'm always surprised when . . .

I can't understand why everyone doesn't take
advantage of this remarkable offer.

. . . this free trial offer.

. . . this no-risk offer.

After all . . .

It costs you nothing.

At the very least, you'll . . .

Yet, of all the _____s who read this message,
only a small percentage will respond.

Maybe you don't believe. . .

. . . or you might feel there's some catch

Maybe you've said to yourself . . .

But maybe there's something else that's
bothering you.

Is that what's holding you back?

I understand your concern.

If that's what you think, please let me set
you straight.

But there's a simple answer.

It's clear that you have nothing to lose.

If you're still not convinced, learn more about
us at _____.com.

For further inspiration, see:
Minimizing Risk

GUARANTEES

Satisfaction guaranteed.
100% satisfaction guaranteed.
Our 100% satisfaction guarantee:
100% satisfaction or your money back.
_____-day no-risk guarantee.
We guarantee your complete satisfaction.
We back it up with our _____ guarantee.
We stand behind our products with a _____ guarantee.
We back all our products with a _____-day guarantee.
Our unconditional money-back guarantee.
Unconditionally guaranteed. Always.
fully guaranteed
quality that's guaranteed
manufacturer's guarantee
lifetime guarantee
lifetime replacement guarantee
You have my promise.
You must be completely satisfied or you pay nothing.
We're not satisfied until you are.
You don't pay for it unless you like it. Period.
We're so confident you'll love _____, we're willing to extend you this _____ guarantee.
This _____ is guaranteed to _____ or you can return it for a full refund.
If you're not completely satisfied, simply return your order within _____ days for a full refund.
If you're not 100% satisfied, just return your _____ within _____ days and owe nothing.
If you decide to return your order, you'll be entitled to a prompt refund or exchange—whichever you prefer.
a full refund, exchange, or credit
If _____ isn't every bit as fantastic as we say it is, simply return it to us within _____ days for a full refund.
You must be 100% satisfied with any item you ever order from us. If not, just return your purchase and we'll promptly send you a full refund.
If I'm not completely satisfied, I will return the _____ for a full refund.
You have my word on it.
I personally guarantee it.
I stake my reputation on it.
I'll see that your money is promptly refunded.
We guarantee that every product in this catalog is truthfully described. If for any reason you are not completely satisfied, simply return your order to us for a full refund. No questions asked.
price protection guarantee
no-hassle returns policy
full-year warranty
lifetime warranty
Your _____ is backed with a _____ warranty.
We guarantee all products for a minimum of _____ days against defects in materials and workmanship.
You won't find this guarantee anywhere else.

For further inspiration, see:
Minimizing Risk

ORDER INFORMATION

Send no money!

Price includes:

Package includes:

Please indicate your choices below.

To send for your _____, just fill out the enclosed postage-paid card and drop it in the mail today.

To order your _____, simply fill out the coupon below and mail it to: _____

Please make payment by check, money order, or credit card.

Charge it!

For even faster service, use your credit card to order by phone. Our 24-hour toll-free number is _____.

To get your _____, call us toll-free at _____. We're open 24 hours a day, 7 days a week.

Our friendly telephone representatives will be glad to assist you.

Just reach for your phone.

Use our toll-free hotline . . .

To shop by phone, . . .

_____ is just a phone call away.

Please have your credit card handy when you call our toll-free number.

Before you call, please fill out the enclosed order form so you'll be ready with all your ordering information.

To order your _____ online, just go to _____.com and click on _____.

Order by phone, fax, or snail mail . . .

Please double-check your order to make sure you've filled in all the information.

Yes! Please send me . . .

Yes! Please enroll me . . .

Yes! I accept your invitation to . . .

Yes! I want to learn about . . .

Yes! I want to enjoy . . .

Yes! I want to _____.

Rush me the . . .

Please accept my order for . . .

Please ship me _____ copies of . . .

Please send me the following items:

I enclose $ _____ in total payment.

Payment enclosed.

Please bill me.

Please bill my _____ (Visa, etc.)

You will be billed in convenient monthly installments.

Your order will be filled promptly.

Your _____ will be on its way . . .

overnight shipping

same-day shipping

Your order will be out our door in 48 hours or less.

Please check the way your name and address appear on the label and make any corrections.

BUSINESS-TO-BUSINESS ONLY

Dealers: See _____ Handbook for discount schedule.
You will be invoiced for the amount shown.
Postage and handling are prepaid and added
  to invoice.
If order amounts to $_____ or less after applicable
  discount, please enclose check or money order
  plus $_____ to cover postage and handling.

New Accounts: Order must total $_____ or more
  after applicable discount to qualify for purchasing on open order.
All orders under $_____ must be prepaid.
Please use official purchase order.

For further inspiration, see:
The Call to Action

FOLLOWING THROUGH

Thank you for writing us . . .

Thank you for your inquiry.

Thank you for your recent request.

Thank you for your interest in _____.

We're delighted to learn of your interest in . . .

You're to be congratulated for your interest in . . .

You couldn't have picked a better time to ask us about . . .

I'm delighted you sent for the information on _____. When you learn the facts, I think you'll be delighted, too.

Here's the information you requested.

Recently we sent you literature on . . .

Recently you signed up for . . .

The _____ you asked for has been sent to you . . .

Your _____ is enclosed.

Thank you for responding to our recent _____.

Thanks so much for enrolling in our...

Thank you for joining _____.

Thanks for choosing _____.

Congratulations! You've made a smart choice.

Welcome aboard!

I'd like to welcome you into the ranks of . . .

We'd like to welcome you into the _____ family.

You've joined over _____ thousand/million other smart _____s who . . .

We're delighted to welcome you as our newest member.

As a member, you now have exclusive access to . . .

Here's how to get started:

To manage or edit your account, simply visit _____.com.

The enclosed literature will fill you in on all the details.

Tell us what you think . . .

Learn more about . . .

If you have any questions, be sure to visit our online FAQ at _____.com.

More questions? Please call us at _____. We're there to help you 24 hours a day, 7 days a week.

We look forward to serving you.

For further inspiration, see:
The Call to Action

PART 4

SPECIAL STRATEGIES

BUILDING OR BASHING AN IMAGE, SELLING YOURSELF, AND MORE

ENHANCING YOUR COMPANY'S IMAGE

our total commitment to . . .
a commitment to excellence
five-star quality
our dedication to . . .
our distinctive style of . . .
knowledge and expertise
over _____ years of experience
We developed . . .
We originated . . .
We created . . .
We pioneered . . .
We're the ones who . . .
We believe in . . .
We question . . .
We challenge . . .
We investigate . . .
We analyze . . .
We search out . . .
We pursue . . .
We uncover . . .
We serve . . .
We uphold . . .
We honor . . .
We affirm . . .
We're dedicated to . . .
We take great pride in . . .
We shaped the growth of . . .
We're committed to . . .

We demand excellence . . .
We meet every challenge . . .
We recognize the realities of . . .
We don't play games with . . .
Day after day, we . . .
At _____, we . . .
Here are just a few of our clients:
What's our formula for success?
Despite what you may have heard, . . .
It's our job to . . .
No other _____ offers you . . .
a stunning variety of . . .
highest quality
unbeatable value
fast, friendly service
prompt delivery
Are we claiming too much? We don't think so.
Who you buy from can be just as important
    as what you buy.
We offer the most comprehensive _____
    in the industry.
We offer the added advantage of . . .
We offer practical, low-cost solutions . . .
We make life easier . . .
We're familiar with every nuance of . . .
The key word is quality.
The _____ name appears only on products
    that meet our high standards.

You're the one who benefits.

The leader in _____ for over _____ years.

The most trusted name in _____.

You can rely on _____ for . . .

our reputation for _____

We worked hard to win our reputation. We work just as hard to keep it.

We've pledged to work harder than ever.

For further inspiration, see:

Heads and Slogans (Part 1)

Distinguished/Status (Part 2)

Experienced/Expert (Part 2)

Reliable (Part 2)

Results/Performance (Part 2)

Service/Help (Part 2)

Superior (Part 2)

JUSTIFYING A HIGH PRICE

_____ may cost more, but it's worth more.

intelligently priced at $_____

Why pay $_____ for a _____, when for a few dollars more, you could have a _____?

for people who can have whatever they want

because you're worth it

Aren't you worth it?

Isn't it better to spend a little more now, instead of a lot more later?

You will be billed in monthly installments of just $_____.

Take a full year to pay.

Your credit is good with us.

_____ will save you money in the long run.

Isn't it worth paying a little extra for _____?

Don't you deserve the best?

the Rolls-Royce of _____

the Harvard of _____

flagrantly expensive, and worth every penny

_____ identifies you as . . .

You probably thought you couldn't afford _____.

You're paying for quality.

pays for itself many times over

The _____ you receive will be worth many times the price.

Allow yourself a little self-indulgence.

Indulge yourself.

a luxury that's within reach

a practical luxury

not as expensive as you think

Treat yourself to a _____.

Pamper yourself . . .

Just this once, let yourself go wild.

a _____ you'll be proud to own

a _____ of obvious distinction

Every distinguished home should have a _____.

For further inspiration, see:

Luxurious (Part 2)

Distinguished/Status (Part 2)

Stylish (Part 2)

Superior (Part 2)

KNOCKING THE COMPETITION

Don't be taken in by . . .

Don't be seduced by . . .

Don't be deceived by . . .

Don't fall for . . .

Don't be fooled by . . .

Don't waste your money on . . .

Our _____ has spawned a host of imitators.

cheap imitations of . . .

pale replicas of . . .

poor substitutes for . . .

clones

knockoffs

wanna-bes

fly-by-night

less reputable

untested

inexperienced

second-rate

inferior

mediocre

cheap

shoddy

slipshod

flimsy

skimpy

substandard

defective

lightweight

no-name

questionable

inadequate

unsound

untested

unproven

inept

incompetent

careless

inaccurate

disreputable

unreliable

unprofessional

phony

bogus

glib

mindless

dull

boring

dreary

monotonous

tedious

inflexible

rigid

slow

sluggish

mind-boggling

complicated

cumbersome

excessive

_____ would have you believe that . . .

inflated claims made by . . .

That might sound fine on the surface, but . . .

a maze of . . .

entangles you in . . .

No other _____ gives you . . .

Unlike other _____s, we . . .

Unlike less reputable _____s, we . . .

_____ is imitated but never equaled.

Accept no substitutes.

Other _____s may try to copy us, but . . .

Other _____s only skim the surface.

We've beaten them at their own game.

We've caught the competition napping.

We offer more _____ than our nearest rival.

Nobody can match our prices.

There's no comparison.

Nobody beats . . .

_____ can't match . . .

_____ can't give you what we do.

Don't settle for less than a _____.

Nothing compares with _____.

No other _____ quite measures up.

No other _____ comes close.

For further inspiration, see:

Enhancing Your Company's Image

Authentic (Part 2)

Competitive (Part 2)

Reliable (Part 2)

Superior (Part 2)

USING DEMOGRAPHICS
TO IMPRESS

What kind of people use (choose/read/buy) _____?
successful people
serious people
people who play as hard as they work
committed to their careers and families
professional
managerial
executive
upwardly mobile
successful
affluent
well-off
financially astute
acquisitive
ambitious
motivated
productive
educated
well-read
bright
intelligent
smart
savvy
curious

independent
young
aware
active
$_____+ HHI (household income)
young spenders
young achievers
trendsetters
_____% are between 25 and 44
_____% hold professional/managerial jobs
_____% own their own homes
_____% earn over $_____
_____% attended college
a highly selective group
key decision makers
a most attractive audience
buying power
impulse buyers
They're a $_____ market.
If you want to score with people like that, . . .

For further inspiration, see:
Distinguished/Status (Part 2)
Superior (Part 2)

FLATTERING
THE READER

You're one of a select few . . .
achievers
doers
leaders
professionals
executives
movers and shakers
community leaders
successful
affluent
influential
thoughtful
smart
intelligent
literate
educated
cultured
discerning
discriminating
generous
concerned
caring
compassionate
principled
outspoken
independent
unconventional
enterprising

progressive
adventurous
trendsetting
creative
spiritual
You've been highly recommended to us.
We extend this invitation to a special few.
You're among the first to receive this
    special offer.
As one of our best customers, . . .
As a responsible citizen, . . .
As a smart _____, you . . .
You have a right to . . .
You demand the best.
You're the toughest critic we know.
You're an active member of your community.
Your education and income set you apart . . .
You're highly selective when it comes to _____.
You're the kind of person who . . .
You're going places.
Your _____ says a lot about you.
You set uncommon goals for yourself.
You're passionate about . . .
You care deeply about . . .
We know that you . . .
for people with high standards
for special people
for men and women of distinction

for those who appreciate the finest _____

for intelligent, influential individuals like you

your discerning taste

a tribute to your taste

_____ celebrates the kind of excellence exemplified by people like you.

This _____ is being sent only to those who fully appreciate . . .

I am inviting you to join a distinguished group of . . .

We refuse to insult your intelligence . . .

For further inspiration, see:

Using Demographics to Impress

Selling Yourself: Personal Traits

Distinguished/Status (Part 2)

SELLING YOURSELF: PERSONAL TRAITS

able	confident	fluent in . . .
accurate	consistent	focused
achiever	cooperative	follow through
act decisively	creative	formidable
active	decisive	friendly
adaptable	dedicated	get along with . . .
addicted to success	demand the best from . . .	goal-oriented
adept	dependable	go-getter
adjust easily to . . .	detail-oriented	good listener
adroit	do whatever it takes	good memory
aggressive	down-to-earth	gregarious
alert	dynamic	hardworking
ambitious	dynamo	healthy
analytical	eager	highly motivated
articulate	easily inspired	honest
attractive	edgy	imaginative
big-hearted	educated	in-depth knowledge of . . .
bilingual	effective	industrious
bold	efficient	ingenious
bright	embrace change	innovative
capable	energetic	integrity
caring	enthusiastic	intelligent
charismatic	executive potential	inventive
clear thinker	experienced	Ivy League
committed to . . .	expert	judicious
communicate effectively	extroverted	leadership ability
compassionate	fast	licensed
competent	fit	likable
computer-literate	flexible	literate

lucid
managerial
maverick
motivated
multilingual
multitalented
negotiator
nonsmoker
open-minded
open to . . .
organized
outgoing
out-of-the-box thinker
outspoken
outstanding
passionate about . . .
patient
people person
perceptive
persevering
personable
plenty of hustle
poised
polished
positive
principled
problem solver

productive
professional
proficient
qualified
quick-thinking
ready
realist
reliable
resourceful
respected
responsible
robust
sane
scholarly
scrupulous
seasoned
self-assured
self-reliant
serious
shrewd
skilled
smart
solid values
sound instincts
sound judgment
spirited
stable

stamina
straight-shooting
strength of character
successful
tactful
talented
team player
tenacious
top-level
trained
trustworthy
upbeat
valuable
versatile
veteran
welcome new challenges
well-educated
well-groomed
well-spoken
willing
witty
work well under pressure
worldly
young
youthful

SELLING YOURSELF: ACHIEVEMENTS

accelerated
accessed
achieved
acquired
acted
administered
advised
advocated
aided
appointed
approved
arranged
assessed
assigned
assisted
attended
authorized
blocked
booked
boosted
brainstormed
broadened
budgeted
built
chaired
challenged
checked
coached
collaborated

competed
completed
conceived
conducted
constructed
consulted
contributed
controlled
converted
coordinated
correlated
counseled
created
delegated
delivered
demonstrated
designed
determined
developed
devised
directed
discovered
doubled
drafted
earned
edited
effected
eliminated
established

evaluated
exceeded
excelled
executed
expanded
expedited
explored
fixed
formulated
founded
fulfilled
generated
guided
handled
headed
helped
hired
identified
implemented
improved
increased
initiated
instituted
instructed
interacted
interviewed
introduced
invented
investigated

launched
led
maintained
managed
marketed
mentored
met with
monitored
motivated
negotiated
nurtured
opened
operated
organized
outlined
outperformed
overcame
overhauled
oversaw
participated
partnered with
performed
pinpointed
planned
prepared
presented
prevented

probed
processed
produced
programmed
promoted
proposed
provided
purchased
questioned
rebuilt
recommended
recruited
reduced
refined
renovated
reorganized
reported
represented
resolved
restructured
reversed
reviewed
revised
revived
saved
scheduled
secured

selected
set priorities
set up
shaped
simplified
sold
solved
spearheaded
steered
streamlined
structured
supervised
supported
tackled
taught
tested
tightened
trained
transformed
trimmed
tripled
upgraded
utilized
won
worked with
wrote

SELLING YOUR IDEAS

acquire
adapt
adopt
advantage
affirm
agree
benchmark
benefit
blueprint
bottom line
brand
breakthrough
capture
communicate
concept
conclude
conducive to
confirm
conservative
cost-effective
cutting edge
decision
decisive
define
demonstrate
departure
design
draft
edgy

efficient
emerge
enhance
enlightened
ensure
envision
evaluate
expanded
expedite
fidelity to
flexibility
focal point
focus
forecast
formulate
forward momentum
fresh
gain
generate
global
hypothesis
idea
ideal
identity
imagination
impact
implement
in tandem with
inaugurate

inclusive
influence
insist
intuitive
investigate
judgment
leverage
management
marginal
maximize
measurable
merit
metaphor
method
minimize
misguided
mission
model
motivate
next level
objective
observe
obsolete
opportunity
option
organization
outline
outside the box
paradoxical

parameters
partner with
pattern
payoff
penetrate
perception
phase
plan
plausible
positioning
positive
possibilities
potential
powerful
precise
preliminary
premise
premium
principles
priority
proactive
process
productivity
professional
profile
program
project
projected
promote
propose
prototype

prove
quest
question
ratio
rational
reap
recoup
reinforce
relevant
reorganize
reputation
residual
resources
response
revamp
revise
revitalize
rigorous
scenario
schedule
scope
seek
solution
solve
sophisticated
stake
stakeholders
status
stimulate
strategy
streamlined

summarize
supersede
surpass
synergy
synopsis
system
target
theory
time-saving
tipping point
tool
transcend
transform
transition
trend
unacceptable
urge
urgent
value
venture
versatile
viable
visibility
vision
wisdom
work flow

For further inspiration, see:
Indispensable (Part 2)
New/Advanced (Part 2)
Results/Performance (Part 2)

"Puffspeak"—And Its Alternative

What follows is a partial listing of inflated words and phrases that have pummeled their way into our language over the objections of writers and other worthy citizens. Some of these terms are elaborate disguises for mundane or unpalatable concepts; others are simply poor usage. Those that I've marked with an asterisk can be safely (even effectively) put to use in your copywriting, but try to assess your audience first.

Puffspeak	Translation
access (used as a verb)*	reach
at this point in time	now
bottom line	What's in it for us?
brand awareness	popularity
Byzantine	scheming, elaborately contrived
cash flow*	income
conceptualize	think
continuum	link
cost-effective	profitable, money-saving
counterproductive*	futile
crisis situation	crisis
downsizing	layoffs
effectuate	bring about
facility	building
finalize	finish
impact (used as a verb)	affect
impact negatively	worsen
income stream	steady income
inoperative	doesn't work
interface (used as a verb)	meet, work with
literally (as in "literally rolling in the aisles")	virtually, practically
leverage (used as a verb)	take advantage of

Puffspeak	Translation
macro-anything	big
mainstreaming	rejoining
mega-anything*	big
meta-anything	(too vague to define; usually implies transcendence, going "beyond")
methodology	rules
mission statement	motto
modality	style
module*	part, unit
nano-anything*	tiny
networking	making connections
normalize	return to normal, stabilize
operational	working
optimal	ideal
optimize	improve
outsourcing	finding cheap replacements for white-collar workers
overriding	major
parameters	limits, guidelines
para-anything	see "meta-anything"
parenting	raising children
parity	equality
prioritize	rank in order of importance
profit center	cash cow
ramifications	consequences
rightsizing	layoffs
scenario	sequence of events
schizophrenic (as in "a schizophrenic foreign policy")	two-faced, conflicting
state-of-the-art*	latest, most advanced
stonewalling	lying
systematize	organize
terminated	finished, fired
time frame	schedule
transpired	happened
upwardly mobile*	successful, affluent

Wordy Expressions

On this list are some prime examples of phrases that amount to little more than "dead wood." Most can be trimmed to a single word.

Avoid	Replace It With
at the present time	now
at this point in time	now
as of this date	now
at that time	then
at that point in time	then
during the time that	when, during
at which time	when, during
on the occasion of	when, during
subsequent to	after
on the grounds that	because
as a result of	because
owing to the fact that	because
accounted for by the fact that	because
by virtue of the fact that	because
owing to the fact that	since
in spite of the fact that	although
with reference to	about
pertaining to	about
in the event that	if
whether or not	whether
the question as to	whether
at an early date	soon
be in receipt of	get
come in contact with	meet
during the time that	while
come to a decision as to	decide

Avoid	Replace It With
reach a conclusion as to	decide
make use of	use
be cognizant of	know
exhibit a tendency to	tend to
give consideration to	consider
in close proximity	near
it is often the case that	often
make an examination of	examine
make mention of	mention
he is a man who	he
this is a subject that	this subject
after very careful consideration	after considering
is of the opinion	believes
make inquiry regarding	inquire

Commonly Misspelled Words

Nothing can subvert the cause of good copy like a well-placed spelling error. The surprising thing is that so many everyday words are packed with opportunities for mistakes. This list, based on U.S. spelling conventions, should help you catch many potential errors before they find their way into print. The best way to use this list is to review it at one or two sittings and jot down on a sheet of paper the words that you typically misspell. Keep your list in plain view until you've committed the spellings to memory.

Note: Parentheses indicate acceptable alternative spellings. In general, the shorter spellings are preferred; e.g., *canceled* takes preference over *cancelled*.

aberration	acrylic	appalling
abridg(e)ment	adaptable	apparatus
absence	adequate	archetype
accede	adjustable	ascertain
accelerate	aerial	assimilate
acceptable	(a)esthetically	associate
acceptance	affiliated	athlete
accessible	ag(e)ing	attendance
accessory	aggressive	awkward
accidentally	alcohol	
acclaimed	alibi	balloon
accolade	allege	bazaar
accommodate	allotment	beggar
accumulate	allotted	believe
accustomed	already	benefit(t)ed
achieve	ambience (-ance)	biased
acknowledg(e)ment	analogous	bicycle
acquainted	analysis	boundary
acquiesce	analyze	boutique
acquire	anonymous	breathe

bulletin
burglar

caffeine
calendar
camouflage
campaign
cancel(l)ed
cancellation
candor
cannot
caress
caricature
casualty
catalog(ue)
category
cemetery
changeable
channel(l)ed
character
chic
chief
choose
cigarette
circuit
clientele
climactic
collaborate
collapsible
colleague
collectible (-able)
colossal
column
commemorate
commission

commitment
committee
compatible
compel
competent
complexion
conceive
conjure
connoisseur
conscience
conscientious
consensus
consistency
contemporary
coolly
copywriter
correspondence
council [group]
counsel [advice, lawyer]
counsel(l)ed
counselor
counterfeit
courteous
cries
cruelly

deceive
decorator
deductible
defense
dependent
description
despair
desperate
deterrent

develop
development
diagram(m)ed
dialogue
dilemma
disappear
disappoint
disastrous
disciplined
disillusioned
dissension
disservice
dissolve
distributor
dubious

ecstasy
eerie
eighth
elegant
embarrass
enclosure
encumbrance
endeavo(u)r
endorsement
entrepreneur
equal(l)ed
exaggerate
exceed
excusable
exercise
exhibitor
exhilarating
existence
exorbitant

extraordinary
exuberant

facsimile
feasible
fiery
flammable
flier (flyer)
fluorescent
focus(s)ed
forecast
foregone
foremost
foresee
foreword [preface]
forgettable
fortieth
forty
forward [ahead]
fries
frivolous
fulfill (-fil)
fulfilled

gaiety
genealogy
gibberish
glamo(u)r
grammar
grievous
guarantee
gullible

handkerchief
harass

height
heroes
hindrance
homogeneous
homogenized
hors d'oeuvre(s)
hungrily
hygiene
hypocrisy

illegible
imperil(l)ed
impostor (-er)
incontestible (-able)
independent
indict
indispensable
ingenious
innocuous
innuendo
inoculate
installed
instilled
intention
iridescent
irrelevant
irreparable
irresistible

jamboree
jeweler
jewelry
judg(e)ment

keenness

khaki
knowledgeable

label(l)ed
laboratory
lacquer
laid
legitimate
leisure
lengthwise
level(l)ed
liable
liaison
license
lik(e)able
likely
liqueur [cordial]
liquor
loathsome
luscious

madam
maintenance
maneuver
marvel(l)ous
mathematics
matinee
meager (-re)
medi(a)eval
medicine
memento(e)s
mileage
milieu
miniature
minuscule (miniscule)

miscellaneous
mischievous
misspell
model(l)ed
monogrammed
mortgage
movable

naive
necessary
negligent
nickel
ninety
ninth
noticeable
nuisance
nutrient

occasionally
occurrence
offense
officially
omelet(te)
omission
oneself
onward
optimism

pageant
paid
panel(l)ed
panicked
parallel
paralyzed
paraphernalia

partisan
pastime
pavilion
perennial
permanent
permissible
perseverance
personnel
picnicking
plaque
plausible
playwright
poignant
possession
potato
potatoes
practice
precede
precious
predecessor
predictable
preferred
preposterous
presence
prestigious
pretense
privilege
procedure
proceed
pronunciation
propeller

quarrel(l)ing
questionnaire
quotient

rarity
receding
receipt
receive
recollect
recommend
reconnaissance
recurrent
registrar
reinforce
reminiscence
remittance
renaissance
reparable
repellent (-ant)
repertoire
resemblance
reservoir
resistance
resource
restaurant
restaura(n)teur
reversible
rhyme
rhythm
rival(l)ed

sacrilegious
salable
satellite
scenery
scissors
scrumptious
secretary
seize

separate
serviceable
shield
shovel(l)ed
silhouette
simultaneously
sincerely
skeptic
smo(u)lder
software
souvenir
specimen
spontaneity
strategy
stratified
strength
stubbornness
stupefying
subtlety
successful
summarize
supersede
surreptitious

synonymous
systematic

terrific
theater (-re)
threshold
tomato
tomatoes
total(l)ed
tranquil(l)ity
transferable
tries
truly
twelfth
tying

vacillate
vacuum
valuable
vehicle
vengeance
veteran
veterinarian

vicious

warehouse
warranty
weird
whims(e)y
wholly
wil(l)ful
wily
wintry
withhold
wondrous
wool(l)en
worsted

yacht
yield
yog(h)urt
yoke
yolk

zany
zigzag

Commonly Confused Words

Our language is filled with deceptive word pairs that seem to exist only to trip up unsuspecting writers. Don't be fooled by outward appearances of similarity. As you'll see on this list, totally unrelated concepts can be disguised as nearly identical twins.

accede—to agree
exceed—to surpass

accept—to receive
except—excluding

adapt—to adjust to
adopt—to accept formally or take as
       one's own

affect—(v) to influence
effect—(v) to bring about, (n) result

aggravate—to make worse
irritate—to tax the nerves

aid—help
aide—staff member

all ready—prepared
already—previously

allusion—reference to
illusion—false image
delusion—false belief

among—more than two involved
between—two involved

appraise—evaluate
apprise—notify

ascent—rise
assent—consent

beside—alongside
besides—also

climactic—pertaining to a climax
climatic—pertaining to climate

complement—complete
compliment—praise

continual—repeated
continuous—uninterrupted

council—(n) a group
counsel—(n) advice, (v) to advise

discreet—cautious
discrete—distinct

disinterested—impartial
uninterested—apathetic

elicit—to draw out
illicit—illegal

elusive—hard to get
illusive—deceptive

eminent—prominent
imminent—in the immediate future

enormity—wickedness, offensiveness
enormousness—giant size

fewer—smaller number of individual items
less—smaller amount by volume

flaunt—to show off
flout—to defy

gibe—jest
jibe—agree *or* jest

imply—to suggest indirectly
infer—to draw a conclusion

it's—contraction of *it is*
its—possessive

loose—unattached
lose—to suffer loss

perquisite—privilege
prerequisite—requirement

precede—to have gone before
proceed—to continue after

premier—top-ranking
premiere—debut

presently—soon
at present—now

principal—chief person or thing
principle—a rule of conduct

sight—something seen
site—place

stationary—motionless
stationery—writing supplies

their—possessive
there—adverb showing location
they're—contraction of *they are*

tortuous—twisting
torturous—excruciating

who's—contraction of *who is*
whose—possessive

you're—contraction of *you are*
your—possessive

Further Reading

Bayan, Richard. *More Words That Sell*. McGraw-Hill, 2003.
Not just more of the same: I've packed this companion volume with lists of words and phrases for fine-tuning and targeting your copy. Use it to reach special niches (business-to-business, fund-raising, financial, subscriptions, technology, classifieds, seniors, young people, and more). Great for adding power and nuance to your general copy, too.

Bly, Robert W. *The Copywriter's Handbook*. Henry Holt, 1990.
A very solid (if marginally outdated) step-by-step guide to the fundamentals of creating effective copy. For print advertising techniques, you can't go wrong with this one.

Bly, Robert W. *The Complete Idiot's Guide to Direct Marketing*. Alpha, 2002.
A first-rate education in the kind of advertising that delivers measurable results, by one of today's top gurus. Yes, it's part of *that* series, but it's surprisingly comprehensive and crammed with helpful tips. Ideal for gaining insight into each form of advertising before you sit down and write.

Caples, John (updated by Fred E. Hahn). *Tested Advertising Methods*, 5th ed. Prentice-Hall, 1998.
Don't let the lackluster title fool you. This is possibly the finest book of its kind ever written, by the legendary pioneer of direct-mail advertising. Timeless wisdom on the psychology and techniques of copywriting for measurable results.

Dahl, Gary. *Advertising for Dummies*. Wiley, 2001.
Essential, easy-to-absorb information for do-it-yourselfers. A good introduction to the business side of advertising, but weak on copywriting.

Glazier, Stephen. *Random House Word Menu*. Random House, 1992.
Nearly a thousand pages of words lists organized by category, compiled by one heroic man. A staggering achievement; great for leisurely browsing as well as quick look-ups.

Godin, Seth. *Permission Marketing*. Simon and Schuster, 1999.
A thoughtful, influential guide to opt-in marketing on the Internet.

Hatch, Denny, and Don Jackson. *2,239 Tested Secrets for Direct Marketing Success: The Pros Tell You Their Time-Proven Secrets.* McGraw-Hill, 1999.
    Anyone who writes direct-response copy can profit from this handy bag of tricks.

Hatch, Denny. *Million Dollar Mailings.* Bonus Books, 2001.
    An expensive but invaluable in-depth look at actual direct-mail winners and what they did right. See if you can find it in the library or persuade your company to purchase it.

Kennedy, Dan S. *The Ultimate Sales Letter: Boost Your Sales with Powerful Sales Letters, Based on Madison Avenue Techniques.* Adams Media, 2000.
    A highly regarded primer on crafting sales letters that hit the mark. Not just a compilation of examples, though it includes lots of them.

Lewis, Herschell Gordon. *Catalog Copy That Sizzles: All the Hints, Tips, and Tricks of the Trade You'll Need to Write Copy That Sells.* McGraw-Hill, 1999.
Lewis, Herschell Gordon. *Direct Mail Copy That Sells!* Prentice-Hall, 1984.
Lewis, Herschell Gordon. *On the Art of Writing Copy: The Best of Print, Broadcast, Internet, Direct Mail.* AMACOM, 2003.
    Lewis is a fascinating contradiction: a maverick spirit who promotes strict adherence to the rules. He habitually lambastes other people's defective copy but still emerges as an insightful, amusing, and very sound teacher. I've listed just a few of his 20 or so books.

Macpherson, Kim. *Permission-Based E-Mail Marketing That Works!* Dearborn Trade Publishing, 2001.
    Practical tips for aspiring online entrepreneurs—ideal in combination with Seth Godin's more conceptual *Permission Marketing.*

Ogilvy, David. *Ogilvy on Advertising.* Vintage Books, 1987.
    Classic advice and insights from the late Madison Avenue legend. Not for agency copywriters only.

Ries, Al, and Jack Trout. *Positioning.* McGraw-Hill, 2001.
    Reprint of an influential work that shows you how to make your product or company stand out from the crowd.

Roget's 21st Century Thesaurus (Princeton Language Institute, ed.). Barnes & Noble Books, 1999.
    When you can't find what you need in my *Words That Sell* books, turn to this indispensable

compendium of synonyms. Going strong since 1852, the venerable Roget's has been updated with a special concept index that makes it even more useful.

Schwab, Victor O. *How to Write a Good Advertisement.* Wilshire, 1980.
    A pre-Internet classic that's simply too good to ignore. Truth never goes out of style.

Strunk, William, and E. B. White. *The Elements of Style.* Allyn & Bacon, 2000.
    Slim, ageless reference guide to English usage and composition, recently updated. Every writer should own it and use it.

Sugarman, Joe. *Advertising Secrets of the Written Word: The Ultimate Resource on How to Write Powerful Advertising Copy from One of America's Top Copywriters and Mail Order Entrepreneurs.* Delstar, 1998.
    Need I say more? A popular guide that covers everything you'd want to know. It's not cheap, so see if your company might order it for you.

Sugarman, Joe. *Triggers: 30 Sales Tools You Can Use to Control the Mind of Your Prospect to Motivate, Influence and Persuade.* Delstar, 1999.
    Another worthwhile book with a long subtitle from that same marketing mastermind.

Trout, Jack, with Steve Rivkin. *Differentiate or Die.* Wiley, 2000.
    More about the art of positioning your product or company to establish a unique identity.

Trout, Jack, with Steve Rivkin. *The New Positioning.* McGraw-Hill, 1996.
    Follow-up to *Positioning*, with emphasis on repositioning in response to change.

Usborne, Nick. *Net Words: Creating High-Impact Online Copy.* McGraw-Hill, 2002.
    Intelligent, in-depth advice on how to shape your writing for the Internet.

Werz, Edward, and Sally Germain. *Phrases That Sell.* McGraw-Hill, 1998.
    Yes, it's a competitor. No, it's not as comprehensive as *Words That Sell*. But you can use this book to expand your collection of time-tested advertising and promotional phrases. Just make sure you buy my *Words That Sell* books first!

KEY WORD INDEX

Can't find a suitable word list to express the concept you have in mind? Use this special index to look up your concept, even if there's no corresponding list for it in this book. The page references will lead you to lists containing words and phrases that convey your idea.

Note: Main topics (and their locations) are printed in **boldface** type.

dramatic, 34–35, 60–61
durable, 32, 51
dynamic, 26, 60–61, 111–112

easy, 28–29, **33**, 39
economical, 53–54, 76
edgy, 34–35, 77, 78–79, 111–112
educated, 77, 108, 109–110, 111–112
educational, 49
effective, 26, 36–37, 62, 63–64, 85
efficient, 28–29, 39, 63–64, 111–112
electrifying, 34–35, 60–61
elegant, 38, 43–44, 50, 77, 78–79, 83
elite, 30–31, 50, 77, 81, 108, 109–110
enchanting/enchantment, 19, 43–44, 58, 65
energy, 26, 34–35, 39, 60–61, 111–112
engaging, 19, 34–35, 41
enjoy/enjoyment, 19, 41, 58
enlightening, 49, 67–68
enriched, 47
entertaining/entertainment, 19, 34–35, 41, 58
essential, 48, 86
ethical, 46, 111–112
exact, 20, 46, 62
excellent/excellence, 36–37, 38, 81, 103
exceptional, 81, 84
exciting, 34–35, 55–56, 60–61
exclusive (elite), 30–31, 81, 84, 108
exclusive (offer), 3–4, 6, 16, 84
exhaustive, 24, 27
exhilarating, 34–35, 41, 58
exotic, 84
expand/expanded, 22–23, 28–29, 47
expensive, 50, 86, 105
experienced, 36–37, 62, 111–112
expert, 36–37, 49, 77, 103, 111–112
exquisite, 38, 43–44, 50, 86
extensive, 22–23, 27
extraordinary, 38, 81, 84
extravagant, 50, 105

fabulous, 38
famous, 30–31, 59
fancy, 50, 78–79, 86
fantastic, 38, 84
fascinating, 34–35, 49
fashionable, 78–79
fast, 33, **39**, 63–64, 82, 111–112
favorite, 59
feminine, 19, 74–75

festive, 41
finest, 50, 81
firm, 32, 70, 74–75
first, 20, 55–56
first-class/first-rate, 30–31, 50, 81
fixes, 63–64
flair, 36–37, 78–79
flexible, 24, 28–29, 85, 111–112
foolproof, 33
foremost, 30–31, 81, 103–104
fragrant, 40, 70
frank, 46
free, 3, 5, 7
freedom, 24
fresh, 19, **40**, 55–56, 57, 84
friendly, 25, 57, 111–112
full-length, 27
fun, 34–35, **41**, 58
functional, 62, 85
funny, 41, 77
futuristic, 55–56

genius, 36–37, 77
genuine, 20, 46, 57, 83
gift, 5, **42**, 80
gifted, 36–37, 77
glamorous, 43–44, 50, 78–79
good-looking, 19, **43–44**, 78–79
graceful, 43–44, 78–79
gracious, 83
great, 22–23, 30–31, 38
greatest, 81
guarantees, 62, 63–64, 66, **97**
guard, 66

handcrafted, 51
handheld, 76
handmade, 50, 51
handsome, 43–44
handy, 28–29, 85
happy/happiness, 41, 58, 67–68
hard-driving, 26, 60–61, 63–64, 111–112
harmonious/harmony, 58, 67–68, 70, 78–79, 80
haunting, 65
healthful, 40, **45**, 57
healthy, 40, 67–68, 111–112
hearty, 40, 57
heirloom, 50, 83
help, 72–73
helpful, 48, 62, 72–73, 85
heritage, 83

high-performance, 55–56, 60–61, 62, 63–64, 77
high-tech, 55–56, 77
hilarious/hilarity, 41
historic, 83
honest, 20, **46**, 57, 111–112
hot (image), 34–35, 38, 59, 74–75, 78–79
hot (temperature), 69
hypnotic, 19, 60–61

ideal, 24, 80
imaginative, 34–35, 36–37, 84, 111–112
immediate, 39, 63–64, 82
important, 30–31, 48, 86
impressive, 22–23, 34–35, 43–44, 60–61, 63–64
improve/improved, 47, 63–64, 67–68
incredible, 38, 60–61, 63–64
in-depth, 27, 49
indispensable, 48, 86
inexpensive, 6, 53–54
influential, 30–31, 36–37, 49, 59, 109
informative, 27, **49**
ingenious, 36–37, 77, 85, 111–112
innovative, 8, 26, 55–56, 111–112
instant/instantly, 28–29, 33, 39, 63–64, 82
instructive, 49
integrity, 46, 57, 111–112
intelligent, 34–35, 77, 108, 109–110, 111–112
intimate, 65, 74–75, 76
intriguing, 34–35
intuitive, 33
investment, 52, 67–68, 86, 89
irresistible, 19

joy/joyous, 19, 38, 41, 58

kiss, 65, 74–75
knockout, 19, 38, 43–44, 78–79

latest, 55–56, 78–79, 82
laugh, 41
lavish, 22–23, 50
leader, 109–110, 111–112
leading, 81, 103–104
legacy, 83
legendary, 30–31, 59, 83
less, 49, **76**
lifesaver, 86
light, 40, 76

spectacular, 22–23, 34–35, 38, 60–61
spiritual, 57, 67–68, 109–110
splendid, 38, 43–44, 50
sporty, 41, 43–44, 78–79
standards, 36–37, 62, 103
star, 59
state-of-the-art, 55–56, 77
status, 30–31, 59, 77, 108, 109–110
steady, 32, 62, 111–112
step-by-step, 33
stimulating, 34–35, 49
straightforward, 33, 46, 57
streamlined, 33, 43–44, 69, 85
strong, 32, 60–61, 111–112
stunning, 34–35, 38, 43–44, 60–61
sturdy, 32
stylish, 77, **78–79**
suave, 77, 78–79
subtle, 69–70, 77, 78–79
success/successful, 30–31, 52, 63–64,
   67–68, 108, 109–110, 111–112
suitable, 80, 85
sumptuous, 50
superb, 38, 50, 81
superior, 30–31, 50, **81**
surefire, 62

talent/talented, 36–37, 77, 111–112
tantalizing, 34–35, 74–75
tasteful, 42, 78–79
tasty, 70

tempting, 19, 34–35, 74–75
tender, 65, 70
tested, 20, 62, 63–64, 66
texture, 69–70
thorough, **27**, 49
thrifty, 53–54
thrilling, 34–35, 60–61
timeless, 83
timely, 39, **82**
time-saving, 28–29, 39, 72–73
tiny, 76
top-ranked/top-rated, 30–31, 81
torrid, 65, 69, 74–75
tough, 26, 32, 46, 60–61
traditional, **83**
trained, 36–37, 72–73, 111–112
tranquil, 25, 66
treasured, 38, 50, 83, 86
tremendous, 22–23, 38, 60–61
trendsetting/trendy, 59, 78–79, 108,
   109–110
trial offer, **7**, 91
trim, 43–44, 76
true, 20, 46, 57, 83
trusted, 46, 62
truthful, 46, 49

ultimate, 27, 34–35, 50, 81
unforgettable, 19, 34–35, 60–61, 83
unique, 80, 84
universal, 85

unlimited, 22–23, 24, 27
unusual, **84**
updated, 47, 55–56, 82
upgraded, 47
upscale, 30–31, 50, 77, 86
up-to-date, 47, 55–56, 82
urgent, 48, 82
useful, **85**
user-friendly, 33

valid, 20, 62
valuable, 5, 48, 50, 72–73, **86**
value, 6, 53–54
vast, 22–23, 24, 27
versatile, 28–29, 80, 85, 111–112
vintage, 83
VIP, 21, 30–31, 77, 109–110
vital, 48, 60–61, 86
vivid, 34–35, 69

warm, 25, 69
wealth, 30–31, 52, 108
wholesome, **40**, 45, 57
win/winner, 5, 59, 67–68
wisdom, 49, 67–68
wise, 52, 77
wonderful, 19, 38
works, 62, 63–64
world-class, 30–31, 81

zesty, 19, 34–35, 41, 70

ABOUT THE AUTHOR

Richard Bayan was advertising copy chief at Day-Timers for 14 years. Previously he served as chief copywriter at Barron's Educational Series and staff writer for Time-Life Books. His work has won the John Caples Creative Award, the American Catalog Award, and the Benjamin Franklin Award, among others. He first broke into print with a series of essays in *National Review* and later joined the staff of *The New American Review*. He is also the author of *More Words That Sell, The Best in Medical Advertising and Graphics, The Cynic's Dictionary,* and over 150 online columns and essays. Mr. Bayan graduated from Rutgers College with a major in history, then earned a master's degree in journalism from the University of Illinois. He currently lives in Philadelphia with his wife and son.